The
POWER
of
THOUGHT

The
POWER
of
THOUGHT

A Twenty-First Century Adaptation of
Annie Besant's Classic Work, *Thought Power*

By
JOHN ALGEO AND SHIRLEY J. NICHOLSON

Quest Books
Theosophical Publishing House

Wheaton, Illinois ◆ Chennai (Madras), India

Quest Books
Theosophical Publishing House
P.O. Box 270
Wheaton, IL 60189-0270

www.questbooks.net

Library of Congress Cataloging-in-Publication Data

Algeo, John.
The power of thought: a twenty-first adaptation of Annie Besant's classic
work, Thought power / John Algeo, Shirley Nicholson.—1st Quest ed.
    p.   cm.
Includes bibliographical references (p. 155).
ISBN 978-0-8356-0797-1
1.   Thought and thinking—Religious aspects—Theosophy. 2. Theosophy—
Doctrines. I. Nicholson, Shirley J. II. Besant, Annie Wood, 1847—1933.
Thought power. III. Title.
BP573.T5 A54 2001
299'.934—dc21   2001025007
                                                              CIP

Printed in the United States of America

CONTENTS

PUBLISHER'S FOREWORD

THE BUDDHA and Heraclitus both said that everything in existence is constantly changing. Books are no exception. Since 1877 books explaining the ideas of the Wisdom Tradition known as Theosophy have been published, and they now exist in large numbers, filled with insights. Publishing such books was one of the early purposes of the Theosophical Society. But because every book is expressed in the language of its time, many of these books, which set forth timeless truths, are expressed in time-bound language. Word choice, grammatical forms, turns of phrase, illustrative examples, length of sentences, order of words, allusions, and even particular factual statements are to some extent out of date. These are superficial matters compared with the deep insights the works contain. Yet, as a consequence, today's readers may have difficulty getting below the surface to the insights beneath. And that difficulty may serve as a barrier between these fine early works and today's readers.

Quest Books, an imprint of the Theosophical Publishing House, has therefore launched a new series of Theosophical classic works reedited and reworked for twenty-first-century readers. Editions in this series aim at preserving the wisdom of the originals, but updating its form of expression by contemporizing the language, the style, and where necessary the content of the originals. These new editions are not intended to, and should not, replace the originals, which will continue to be available for those who prefer them, as well as for historical purposes and as benchmarks by which to judge these and future editions. In time the present reedited versions will themselves need to be replaced with yet newer versions based on the originals. Change is no cause for concern, but a failure to respond to change is.

The adapters of this book make no claim to or for its original content, for which the original author alone is responsible. The adapters' aim has been to make that content as accessible as possible, and they alone are responsible for omissions, changes, and additions made to the original text in pursuit of that aim.

We hope that the volumes in this new series of Quest Books will introduce old wisdom to new readers and in some cases entice them to examine the originals and explore further in the limitless expanse of Theosophy.

The
POWER
of
THOUGHT

I *think; therefore I am.*
    —René Descartes

It *is probable that the psyche and matter are two*
different aspects of one and the same thing.
    —C. G. Jung

It *is only through a vehicle of matter that*
consciousness wells up as "I am I."
    —H. P. Blavatsky

Chapter One

THE POWER OF THOUGHT
AND OF THE THINKER

CHAPTER SUMMARY

*Thought is power by which we know the world around us
and other people. And by our thought we affect the
world for good or for ill.*

*Thought also gives us the capacity to know ourselves. And by
our thought we can recreate ourselves.*

*The right use of all knowledge is to improve life for ourselves
and others.*

The thinker is a conscious self working in matter.

*Consciousness and matter are the two expressions of the
ultimate One Reality, the source of all that is and the
potential source of all that can be.*

*Each of us is a "self"—a quantum or ray of consciousness
of the One Self, Primordial Consciousness, or One
Reality.*

*As a self, we function by knowing, willing, and energizing
matter—from which arise thoughts, desires, and
actions.*

Chapter One

The "not-self" is the self's perception of everything outside itself, including all other separated selves as well as our own thoughts, desires, and physical bodies.

The relationship between the self (or knower) and the not-self (or that which is known) is "knowing":

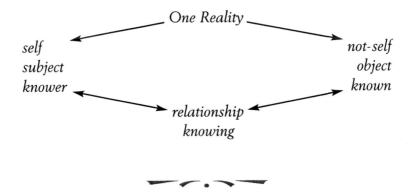

THOUGHT IS POWER—real power, objective power. It is not just something subjective in our heads. Our thoughts have energy and a kind of material reality by which they affect other people and color the mental atmosphere around us.

We can learn to use the power of thought to make ourselves a positive force in the world by helping others. We can use this power to discover who we really are, thus fulfilling the ancient command to "Know yourself." We can use this power to develop what is best in our nature and so achieve a fuller, more productive, happier, and more useful life. This short book can help us to utilize better the powerful energy of our thoughts and our thinking.

We share our world with all other living beings. The very air we breathe in and out is air that others all around us have already breathed. It has already been in the lungs and bloodstreams of countless others, and each organism that uses the air modifies it by taking something out of it and adding something to it. Animals take out oxygen and add carbon dioxide; plants reverse the process. And each of us may add microorganisms, such as flu bugs, to the air we breathe. So with every breath, we take into ourselves something of all the other breathing creatures on this planet. In sharing the same air, we share ourselves with others.

We live, however, not just in a physical environment, but also in emotional, mental, and other environments. We influence all those environments, and they in turn influence us, just as much as we and our physical surroundings are mutually influential. Our planet's atmosphere includes not only the physical air, but also emotions and thoughts. We live in an atmosphere of feeling and thinking just as surely as we live in an atmosphere of gasses. The total ecology of our planet thus has physical, emotional, and mental dimensions.

We can think of those nonphysical environments as worlds made of kinds of matter that are subtler than the physical stuff around us and not perceptible through our sense organs—but matter nonetheless. Feelings and thoughts are forms in that nonphysical matter. And just as we can make and unmake forms in the physical world, so we can make and unmake those emotional and mental forms. All of us are continually modifying our shared subtle environment as well as our physical one. We can learn to shape our world consciously and deliberately.

Thought is a creative power. It makes actual forms in the thought atmosphere around us that affect the way we and others habitually respond to the world. Thus a knowledge of how the power of thought operates can help us to understand the world around us and to find meaning in life. Knowledge about how thought works can also lead us to recognize the limits of what we know and to realize that we do not perceive things as they really are. It can help us relate to others and gain self-knowledge.

Our ultimate ignorance is not knowing who *we* are. Philosophical and religious traditions throughout human history have called that knowledge the most important thing in the world. Over the entrance to the temple at Delphi, the Greeks inscribed the motto "Know thyself." The great Hindu philosophical treatises of the Upanishads say that knowledge of our own identity lets us know everything else we need to know. Alexander Pope in *An Essay on Man* wrote, "All our knowledge is ourselves to know." If we do not know who or what we are, we cannot value ourselves or do anything right. As Tennyson wrote in his poem *Oenone*:

> Self-reverence, self-knowledge, self-control,
> These three alone lead life to sovereign power.

Knowing who we are (self-knowledge) lets us understand our worth (self-reverence) and the way to use the power latent within us (self-control) for the benefit of the whole world, including ourselves (sovereign power).

How can we gain self-knowledge? If someone asks us who we are, we are likely to respond with our name or information about our occupation, family relationships, and other such external facts. But those facts certainly do not get at the core of us. If *we* ask ourselves who we are, the answer may be harder to come by. We may not know who we are. One aim of this book is to help its readers use the power of thought to answer that most important question, "Who am I?"

Part of the insight we need to answer that question is learning the difference between our self as thinker and the thoughts we create, which have a kind of life of their own. This book suggests ways to gain power over our thoughts rather than letting them have power over us. It teaches us to free our capacity for thought by learning to concentrate and deliberately to use thought for good ends. It shows how powerful thought can be when applied to making life better, fuller, and more satisfying. This practical knowledge is based on a particular way of looking at our own nature and the nature of the world around us.

The materialist view that dominates ordinary Western science regards thought as a byproduct of the brain. That view is captured in the nineteenth-century epigraph: "The brain secretes thought as the stomach gastric juice, the liver bile, and the kidneys urine." That statement—grossly materialistic as it is—contrasts with one by an early expounder of Theosophy, Kuthumi Lal Singh: "Thoughts are things." Despite the superficial likeness between the two statements in their shared assertion of the materiality of thought, the two views are metaphysically worlds apart because Theosophy also acknowledges a thinker—a self—who generates the things that are thoughts.

As he thinks in his heart, so is he.
—Proverbs 23.7

Chapter One

Man is but a reed,
the most feeble thing in nature,
but he is a thinking reed.

—Blaise Pascal

THE SELF AS KNOWER

In studying human nature, we need to distinguish our inner self (our core essence, which is who we really are) from the "vehicles" or "bodies" we use. We normally think of our bodies as ourselves, but as we will see, our bodies are in fact aspects of the not-self. As mentioned above, there are many sorts of matter in the world in addition to the dense physical stuff we experience through our senses; and we have bodies composed of each of those sorts of matter. The various sorts of matter are sometimes called "planes" of matter (though that is a metaphor and they are not two-dimensional or layers). They are sometimes described as "fields" because they do not have the kind of solidity and density we associate with physical matter and bodies made of it. Here we are concerned with five sorts of matter and the bodies we use that are made of each of them. These bodies are the non-self that the self experiences most directly:

1. the dense physical, which is what we ordinarily understand as our body,

2. the vital (also called "etheric"), which is a subtler counterpart of the physical and is closely related to it as the channel of our life energy,

3. the emotional (also called "astral"), which embodies desires, fears, and all other feelings,

4. the lower or concrete mental, what we normally think of as our mind, our thinking function, closely connected with emotions, vitality, and the physical brain,

5. the higher or abstract mental (also called "causal"), which is the body for our essential self of individual identity, which links our repeated incarnations together despite their different lower mental, emotional, etheric, and dense physical bodies.

Each of these bodies is made of a characteristic kind of matter, subtler than that of the preceding one. Each kind of matter constitutes a "plane" or "field." Together, the etheric, emotional, lower mental, and higher mental bodies form what is sometimes called the human "aura." They have been described as spheres of light surrounding and interpenetrating the physical body, which anchors them to the dense physical world.

If we think of these bodies in terms of Jungian psychology, the dense physical is the channel for sensations; the etheric is the channel for the flow of the libido or vital energy; the emotional is the channel for feelings; the lower mental is the channel for thinking; and the higher mental is the channel for intuitions and for contacting the collective unconscious.

We are none of those bodies, but we act, live, feel, think, and intuit through them. "We"—our core self—is a unit of consciousness emanated from the one primordial consciousness, the One Self or God (called the "Logos" in

Greek), as a ray of light shines forth from the sun or a quantum is part of the infinite radiant energy of the universe. As this core self, we function through our causal body by knowing, willing, and energizing the world around us; and from those functions come thoughts in our mental body, desires in our astral body, and actions in our physical and etheric bodies.

We don't usually consider the stuff of thoughts and desires to be matter, but that is exactly what it is in this view. These kinds of matter are much subtler and more tenuous than physical stuff, but they are matter all the same. We live in a world of interpenetrating fields—dense, etheric, emotional, mental, and causal. It's all there at once, all around us. And all these forms of matter are variations of a basic root-stuff or primal matter, just as solids, liquids, and gasses are all variations of the same physical particles. We don't know that basic root-stuff directly any more than we do the primordial consciousness; we know both only through their manifestations in the world around us and in ourselves.

Just as physical things are made out of dense physical matter—mountains, apple trees, and squirrels—so too emotional and mental things are made out of emotional and mental matter. We are surrounded by emotional and mental environments, just as we are by a physical environment. We have an emotional and a mental body through which we feel and think, just as we have a physical body through which we act. And there are emotional and mental forms in the emotional and mental environmental atmospheres all around us, just as there are physical forms like mountains, apple trees, and squirrels in the physical environment around us.

*We are slowly recovering . . . the knowledge
which was universal in the ancient world,
that there is no such thing as matter
apart from mind or consciousness.*
—Father Bede Griffith

In our essence, however, we are none of this. We are no more our mental bodies than we are our physical bodies. We are a focus of consciousness, a self, that knows it exists. But the self trying to perceive itself is like an eye trying to see itself. Yet the self is that consciousness—that conscious, feeling, ever-existing awareness—by which we each know that we exist.

We can never think of ourselves as nonexistent or believe "I am not." The self-affirmation "I am" stands before and beyond all argument. No proof can make it stronger; no disproof can weaken it. Both proof and disproof are based on the recognition of "I am," the unanalyzable feeling of existence, of which nothing can be predicated except increase and diminution. "I am more" is the expression of pleasure; "I am less" is the expression of pain. But "I am" is the given fact.

When we observe this "I am," we find that it expresses itself in three different ways. First, it knows, that is, it reflects within itself things that are outside itself; from the viewpoint of the separate self, each of those outside things is a not-self, something other than the self of the knower.

Those not-selves include all the mountains, apple trees, and squirrels in the world, as well as all the nebulas and molecules; they also include all other selves that are not ourselves. So the "I am" knows and says "I think." Second, the "I am" wills and says "I desire." And third, the "I am" energizes and says "I act." These are the three affirmations of the essential self, the "I am."

The self manifests in our worlds in just these three ways: thinking, desiring, and acting. As all the infinite colors of the spectrum arise from the three primary ones, so the numberless expressions of the self all arise from knowledge, will, and energy, expressed in thinking, desiring, and acting. These are powers inherent in human nature that are brought from latency and improved through evolution.

The self as knower, the self as willer, the self as energizer—they are the One Self in eternity and are also the root of our individuality in time and space. Our present concern, however, is especially with the self as knower. And that leads to taking a closer look at the difference between "self" and "not-self."

The thoughts that come often unsought,
and, as it were, drop into the mind,
are the most valuable of any we have,
and therefore should be secured,
because they seldom return again.
—John Locke

THE NOT-SELF AS THE KNOWN

The world as we perceive it in its five levels of matter contains just two things: our self and everything else, the self and the not-self. This perception reflects an important metaphysical principle.

Western materialism has adopted the principle that dense physical matter is the fundamental reality in the world and that everything, including consciousness and thought, is either a form or a secondary effect of that matter, an "epiphenomenon." The view here is quite different: the underlying Reality has two poles, matter and consciousness, just as a magnetized bar has positive and negative poles. Reality itself is a third unknowable something different from either matter or consciousness, but from which they both arise and in which everything that can be is latent. We can call it the "One Reality," but like the Chinese sage Lao Tzu, we cannot say anything about it: "The way that can be talked about is not the real Way; the name that can be spoken is not the real Name." Like the voice Moses heard from the burning bush, it only says to us, "I am." Because it is potentially everything, we can say nothing else about it, for to say that it is this or that would be to limit it.

Though we cannot define it, we experience that One Reality both as consciousness and as matter. The conscious aspect of the world is also called "the life side," and the material aspect "the form side." The consciousness inside us is our essential "self"; the matter all around, including our five bodies, is "not-self."

Though they both inhere in the One Reality, the conscious self in us is a knower and what it knows is the not-self. The relationship between these two poles is knowing. That knowing is supremely important because it is the way we come into contact with other selves, and it is also a way we come to the knowledge of ourselves, of who we are. Knowledge of the not-self is gained by thinking, and thinking can also help us come to self-knowledge—the most important thing in the world.

The power of thought is useful for achieving all sorts of practical, mundane things in our personal lives. It can make us happier, more effective, better in our jobs and relationships, more satisfied with our lives. And such use of thought power is one subject of this book. But the most important use of thought power is to help us discover who we are and how we relate to the not-self around us. That is the primary focus of this book.

We begin by distinguishing our "self" from the "not-self." As already suggested, the not-self includes mountains, apple trees, and squirrels, but also our own fivefold bodies. The self is the knower, and our bodies—physical, etheric, emotional, mental, and causal—are the most intimate and immediate part of the not-self we can gradually come to know.

The power of thought—the magic of the mind.
—Byron

The mind is its own place, and in itself
Can make a heaven of Hell, a hell of Heaven.
—John Milton

Knowing

The knower, the known, the knowing—these are the three aspects of a single process that we must understand before we can use our thought power effectively and productively. According to common Western philosophical terminology, our consciousness or self is the "subject" that knows; the world around us, the not-self including our five bodies, is the "object" that is known. The relationship between them is the process of knowing. In this process, the not-self affects the self, and the self in turn affects the not-self. Knowing is a mutual interchange between our self and all the not-selves we are aware of. We must understand the nature of the knower or self, the nature of the known or not-self, and the mutual relationship between them. We also need to understand how that relationship arises.

When we have understood these things, we will have made a step toward the self-knowledge that is wisdom. Then, indeed, we will be able to aid the world around us, becoming its helpers and even its saviors. We are all interconnected in the same environments—physical, emotional, and mental—so whatever we do helps or harms all others. The true end of wisdom, motivated by love, is to help lift the world out of misery into the knowledge by which all pain ceases forever. That is the object of all true study; the proper use of philosophy is to put an end to pain. Wisdom is that which leads us to peace. For that purpose, the knower thinks; for that purpose, we continually seek knowledge.

APPLICATIONS

1. Is the statement in the box below true or false?

> **Every statement in this box is false.**

This is an old puzzle known as the paradox of the liar. On the one hand, if the statement is true, then it is false. On the other hand, if it is false, then it is true. What makes the paradox and what resolves it? How is a statement that is about itself like a self trying to identify itself?

2. Make a list of ten roles you play in life, such as your occupation, sex, nationality, ethnicity, religion, marital status, family relationships, hobbies, avocations, and so on. Then chose one of these which seems to be most prominent. Now close your eyes and imagine yourself without this role. What does it feel like? In imagination, eliminate the other roles, one by one. What is left? Can you sense the "real you" who plays all the roles in your life?

3. Close your eyes and relax for a few minutes while you let your thoughts wander wherever they will go as you observe them. Then deliberately focus your mind on something—the image of a tree, the face of someone you love, a quotation you remember, a problem you need to solve. Now open your eyes and compare the two experiences. When your thoughts drifted, you experienced thoughts as things in your mental body with a life of their own. You did not think them; they thought you. When you focused your mind, you functioned as the thinker, the consciousness that can control your thoughts. In these two mental modes, you can sense the difference between yourself as thinker and the objects of your thought.

4. For more information about the Theosophical view of the human constitution and mind, consult *Man and His Bodies*, *The Seven Principles of Man*, and *A Study in Consciousness* by Annie Besant.

Mind moves matter.
—Virgil

Thought forms in the soul in the same way clouds form in the air.
—Joseph Joubert

A man is but the product of his thoughts; what he thinks, he becomes.
—Mohandas K. Gandhi

Chapter Two

THE NATURE OF THOUGHT

CHAPTER SUMMARY

Thought can be considered from the standpoint of life (spirit, consciousness) or of form (matter, body).

When the self "knows" some object or "not-self," it has reproduced an image of that object in the matter of its mental body.

Everything in manifestation is in motion, and regular rhythmic motion is vibration.

Each self (or unit of consciousness) is enclosed in various material bodies, whose vibrations are communicated through intervening matter to the bodies of other selves. By this network of communication, selves can know one another.

Different forms of matter—mental, emotional, physical— have different characteristic vibrations resulting in thoughts, desires, and actions.

Chapter Two

*Our consciousness... by its selective faculties
of perception and co-ordination determines the
type of world in which we live. A different kind
of consciousness would create a different world
around us, whatever the raw material
of the universe may be.*
—Lama Anagarika Govinda

THOUGHT CAN BE CONSIDERED from two standpoints: from the side of the self, which is the knower
that is conscious of knowledge, or from the side of the
known or the ever changing forms, whose changes make
knowledge possible. The contrast of the two standpoints
has led to two extremes in philosophy, each of which
ignores one side of Reality. One view (sometimes called
"idealism") regards everything as consciousness, ignoring
the need for form to condition consciousness and make it
possible. The other (called "materialism") regards everything as form, ignoring the fact that form can exist only
because consciousness or life ensouls it. Any philosophy
that tries to explain everything from only one of those
standpoints is doomed to problems it is unable to solve.

Life and form, spirit and matter, consciousness and
body, are inseparable in manifestation. They are the indi-
visible aspects of what Indian philosophers call "That,"
the One Reality. That One Reality is neither consciousness nor matter, but the root of both. Consciousness and
its bodies, life and form, spirit and matter, are the tempo-

rary expressions of the two aspects of the one unconditioned Existence. That unconditioned Existence manifests
as Root Spirit and Root Matter. Root Spirit (called
pratyagātman in Sanskrit) is abstract Being, the Logos
or conscious Reason governing the universe, from which
all individual selves come. Root Matter (*mūlaprakriti* in
Sanskrit) is primal substance, the source of all forms.

Whenever manifestation takes place, Root Spirit and
Root Matter give birth respectively to all individual units
of consciousness and all the diverse forms of matter.
Beneath these two Roots is the One Reality, forever in-
cognizable by our ordinary consciousness. The flower
does not see the root from which it grows, even though it
draws all its life from that root, without which the flower
could not be.

The characteristic function of the self as knower is to
mirror within itself the not-self. An analogy is a photo-
graphic film that receives light reflected from objects.
This light causes modifications in the sensitized surface
on which it falls, producing images of the objects. It
is similar with our essential self as the knower of the
external world. The knower's
vehicle (the mind or men-
tal body) is like a spher-
ical mirror on which
the self receives re-
flected light from
the not-self, causing
images to appear on
the sphere's surface.
These images are the
reflections of that which
is not the self.

Chapter Two

In ordinary states of consciousness, the knower does not know things as they are, but only by the images they produce in the mind. Hence the mind, the vehicle of the self as knower, has been compared to a mirror, in which we see the images of all objects placed before it. A mirror seems to have the objects within it, but those objects we see are only images, illusions caused by the light reflected from the objects. So the mind, in its reflection of the outer universe, knows only the illusive images and not the things in themselves. The self as knower mistakes these mental images for external objects.

Mistaking the images in our minds for external reality is called "maya" in Hindu philosophy, where the traditional example is of a person who goes into a dark room and thinks a cobra is coiled in a corner, ready to strike. But when the person strikes a light, what looked like a cobra in the dark is revealed as only some loops of rope. The reflection is not the reality; the map, as the General Semanticists say, is not the territory. Our perceptions are always inaccurate reproductions of actuality.

Now, the analogy of the mirror and the use of the word "reflection" in the preceding paragraphs are a little misleading, for mental images are actually *reproductions* not *reflections* of the objects that cause them. As already explained, the mind is composed of a rarefied kind of matter. Part of the matter of the mind is actually shaped into a likeness of the object presented to it, and the knower becomes conscious of this likeness, called a "thought form." When we as knower thus modify part of our mental body into the likeness of an external object, we *know* that object. But the image is never a perfect reproduction of the object, for the reason alluded to above and treated in the next chapter, and so our knowledge is always flawed.

The mind of man may be compared to a musical instrument with a certain range of tones, beyond which in both directions we have an infinitude of silence.

—John Tyndall

But, it may be asked, will that always be the case? Can we never know things fully in themselves? That question brings us to the vital distinction between consciousness and the matter in which consciousness is working, and by this distinction we may find an answer to the question.

Our present life is only one in a long series of incarnations, repeated rebirths by which we evolve physically, emotionally, mentally, and spiritually. When, after many lives and long evolution, our consciousness has finally developed the power to reproduce within itself all that exists outside it (that is, to know everything), then the envelope of causal matter in which it has been working falls away. It has served its purpose of serving as a link between incarnations, the "cause" of our succeeding personalities, and is no longer needed.

Then the consciousness as knower identifies itself with all the other selves among which it has been evolving. It is no longer a totally separate self, but realizes its underlying unity with them as complementary expressions of the Reality behind the one Root Spirit or primordial consciousness of the universe. And then it sees as the not-self only matter connected with all selves alike.

In her major work, *The Secret Doctrine*, H. P. Blavatsky calls this the "Day Be-With-Us," the union which is the triumph of evolution, when the consciousness in one self knows itself as all others, and knows all others as itself. By their sameness of nature, all selves attain perfect knowledge and realize that marvelous state where identity does not perish and memory is not lost, but where separation ends. Knower, knowing, and knowledge are then one. But that is a long time in the future.

Meanwhile, we are evolving, among other ways, by expanding our knowledge; and we have to study the nature of thought in order to understand how we do this. We need to see clearly the illusory side of the world around us and of our own nature as separate, isolated selves. We have to understand the illusion before we can transcend it. So now we turn to the nature of thought and to how knowing—the relation between the knower and the known—arises.

THE CHAIN OF KNOWER, KNOWING, AND KNOWN

Motion, which is change or becoming, is the root of everything that exists. Modern science now tells us, as Eastern wisdom always has, that vibration or frequency pervades all nature. Life is motion; consciousness is motion. And motion affecting matter is vibration.

Philosophers have thought of the One, the All, as changeless, either as absolute motion or as motionless. Relative motion—that is, the motion of each thing in relationship to every other thing—cannot exist in the One, which is a unity without parts. Relative motion is a change of relationship in space between two things. Absolute motion is the presence of every moving unit at every point of space at every moment of time—everything potentially everywhere, but nothing actually anywhere. Paradoxically absolute motion is identical with motionless rest, being only rest looked at in another way.

Only when there is differentiation, or parts, can we think of what we call motion. When the One becomes the many, then relative motion arises. The essence of matter is separateness and multiplicity, as that of spirit is unity. Matter and spirit separate out of the One, as cream and skim milk separate from unhomogenized whole milk. When matter and spirit thus separate, the omnipresence of the One is reflected in the multiplicity of matter as ceaseless and infinite motion. From the standpoint of spirit there is always One; from that of matter there are always many. As mentioned in the first chapter, the One has everything within it; so it is potentially everywhere, and thus motionless, whereas the manifested many are actually here or there and moving.

When this infinite motion appears as rhythmical movements in matter (vibrations or frequencies), it is health, consciousness, vitality. When motion is irregular and without rhythm, it is disease, unconsciousness, death. Life and death are twin sisters, alike born of motion, which is manifestation.

All matter depends on motion.
—René Descartes

Chapter Two

Each unit of consciousness is isolated from all the other units by the enclosing walls of matter of its five bodies. "A separated unit of consciousness" is here called a "self" (with a small "s") to distinguish it from the One Self (with a capital "S"), which is the source of all consciousness. (In Sanskrit the separate unit is called a *jīva*.) Each self becomes embodied in, or expresses itself through, the five vehicles of matter mentioned above. As these vehicles vibrate, they communicate their vibrations to the matter surrounding them, and this surrounding matter becomes the medium by which the vibrations are carried outward.

The surrounding matter, in turn, communicates the impulse of vibration to the enclosing vehicle of another self, and thus causes that self to vibrate like the first. The result is a chain of vibrations by which one unit of consciousness knows another. The second self knows the first because it reproduces the vibrations of that first in itself, and thus experiences as that first one experiences.

Yet a discrepancy or an asymmetry arises because the second self is already in a vibratory condition. After it has received the impulse from the first self, the second self's state of motion is not a simple repetition of that impulse, but a combination of its own original motion with that imposed from without. Hence the reproduction is not perfect. Similarities can be obtained, ever closer and closer ones, but complete mutual identity always eludes us, as long as the vehicles remain.

This sequence of vibratory actions is often seen in nature. A flame is a center of vibratory activity. Its heat adds energy to the surrounding air molecules, increasing their random motion, and the air temperature rises. This increased motion speeds up the rate of movement in the molecules in a piece of iron lying nearby. Its particles vibrate faster under the impulse, and so the iron becomes hot and a source of heat in its turn. So also vibrations pass from one self to another, and all beings are thus interlinked by the network of connections.

Ranges of Vibration

In physical nature we mark off different ranges of vibrations or frequencies by different names, calling one set of vibrations light, another heat, another electricity, another sound, and so on. Yet all are of the same nature, being modes of motion, although they differ in frequency and in the character of their waves. Similarly, thoughts, desires, and actions—the active manifestations in matter of knowledge, will, and energy—are also made up of vibrations that differ in the phenomena they produce because of their different vibrational character. Vibrations in a particular kind of matter and with a certain character are called thoughts; vibrations of another series are spoken of as desires; another series of vibrations are actions.

What we call a mind is nothing but a heap or collection of different perceptions, united together by certain relations, and supposed, though falsely, to be endowed with a perfect simplicity and identity.
—David Hume

27

Just as our eyes respond to certain electromagnetic frequencies called light, our mind responds to other far subtler frequencies unknown to physical science, which we call thought. "Seeing" occurs when certain electromagnetic frequencies from an object reach our eye; "thinking" occurs when the thought field between an object and our mind is thrown into waves. The one is not more—nor less—mysterious than the other.

Thought waves have an impact on the subtle matter of which the mind is composed by modifying the way in which that matter is arranged. In sensory or concrete thinking, we replicate original impacts that come from without. The knower interacts with these vibrations; and the result is knowledge. A thought is a reproduction within the knower's mind of that which is not the knower or self; it is a picture, caused by a combination of wave motions, quite literally an image. A part of the not-self vibrates; as the knower vibrates in response, that part becomes the known; the matter quivering between knower and known makes knowing possible by putting the two into touch with each other. Thus the chain of knower, known, and knowing is established and maintained.

APPLICATIONS

1. Cup your hands around, but not touching, a glowing electric light bulb. Explain what enables you to know that the bulb is "on" even if you do not see it. How does that knowledge reach you? How is this analogous to the way we come to know other things in the world?

2. For illustrations of how images are reproduced in our subtle bodies, look at plates 5, 8, 11, 14, and 14a, and read the accompanying texts in *The Personal Aura*, by Dora van Gelder Kunz.

What is my spiritual practice?
Highlighting passages in books.
— Joseph Campbell

Much of man's thinking is
propaganda of his appetites.
—Eric Hoffer

A great many people think they are
thinking when they are merely
rearranging their prejudices.
—William James

A man may dwell so long upon a thought
that it may take him prisoner.
—Marquis of Halifax

Chapter Three

THE CREATOR OF ILLUSION

CHAPTER SUMMARY

The mind is the tool that the conscious self uses for perceiving and responding to the world, but it also limits and distorts our contact with the world.

If we are aware of the limitations of the mind—which create illusions—we can allow for them and not be misled by them.

We have shaped the mind we now have by the ways we have used it in the past, and we can change it, but only slowly and with effort.

One way to change our mind is to associate with persons whose minds are more like what we want ours to be, but change comes best from active effort, not passive reception.

Chapter Three

*Having become indifferent to objects of percep-
tion, the pupil must seek out the Raja of the Senses,
the Thought-Producer, he who awakes illusion.
The Mind is the great slayer of the Real.*

So H. P. BLAVATSKY writes in her prose poem *The Voice
of the Silence*, which she translated from an Eastern
source called "The Book of the Golden Precepts" as one
of her last gifts to the world. And there is no more significant description of the mind than that which awakes
or creates illusion.

The mind is not the knower or self, so we should
always be careful to distinguish the two. Many difficulties
arise if we confuse that which knows (the knower) with
the mental body, which is the instrument for obtaining
knowledge. It is as though a sculptor were identified
with a chisel.

The mind (or *manas*, which is how consciousness
functions through mental matter) is fundamentally dual.
It is made up of two aspects: (1) the "abstract" mind,
which functions through finer grades of mental matter,
called the causal body, and (2) the "concrete" mind, which
functions through relatively coarser grades of mental
matter, called the mental body. The mind itself is a reflection in matter of that aspect of the self that knows,
the knower.

The mind is at the same time both a source of information and a limitation on what we can know. Several
comparisons make this point. Our mind is our window
onto the world. But a window does two things at once. It
is an opening to the wider world around us, penetrating
the wall of our isolation. But it also limits what we can see

because it opens in only one direction and gives us only one view. So the mind lets the self know the not-self, but limits that knowledge to what it can receive.

Another comparison is the well-known story from the Jains in India about five blind men who wanted to find out what an elephant was like. Each of them felt with his hands the part of the elephant he first encountered: flank, leg, tail, tusk, or trunk. Because of that difference, they thought that an elephant was very much like, respectively, a wall, a tree, a rope, a spear, and a snake.

A third comparison also has to do with touch. If, for some reason, we put on thick gloves, the gloves would deprive our hands of much of their power of feeling, sensitivity of touch, and ability to pick up small objects. We are then capable of grasping only large objects and of feeling heavy impacts. So it is with the knower who puts on the mind. The hand is there as well as the glove, but its capacities are greatly lessened; the knower is there as well as the mind, but its powers are severely limited in expression.

VIBRATIONS AND THE CONCRETE MIND

The term "mind" is used here for the concrete mind— the consciousness working through the mental body. This mind has been conditioned by past thinking and is constantly being modified by present thinking. It has certain capacities and limitations, strengths and weaknesses, which result from our activities in previous lives. Our mind is as we have made it. We cannot change it except slowly; we cannot transcend it by a simple effort of the will; we cannot cast it aside or instantaneously remove its limitations. Such as it is, it is ours, a part of the not-self that we as knowers have appropriated and shaped for our own use. Only through it can we know the world around us.

All the results of our past thinking are present in our mind as conditioning, and each mind has its own rate and range of vibration. Each mind is in a state of perpetual motion, offering an ever-changing series of pictures. Every impression from outside appears on this already active mirroring sphere, and the many existing vibrations modify and are modified by each newly arriving vibration. The result is not, therefore, an accurate reproduction of the new vibration, but a combination of it and already existing vibrations.

To use again an analogy from light, if we hold a piece of red glass before our eyes and look at green objects, they appear to us to be black. The vibrations that give us the sensation of red are cut off by those that give us the sensation of green, and the eye is deceived into seeing the object as black. So also if we look at a blue object through a yellow glass, we see it as black. In every case a colored medium causes an impression of color different from that of the object when looked at by the naked eye.

The influence of the mind as a medium by which the knower views the external world is very similar to the influence of a colored glass on the colors of objects the eye sees through it. Even looking at things with the naked eye, we see them somewhat differently from what they are because the eyes, the optic nerve, and the brain modify the vibrations more than we are aware. The knower is as unconscious of this influence of the mind as a person who sees only through red or blue glasses would be unconscious of the effect of the glasses on the colors of an object.

The mind is called the "creator of illusion," because it presents us with only distorted images, a combination of itself and the external object. But in a far deeper sense, it is, indeed, the "creator of illusion," in that even these distorted images are but images of appearances, not of realities. For example, the eye sees only light that bounces off an object, not the object itself. But physicists tell us that objects themselves are different from anything we suppose. So shadows of shadows are all that the mind gives us. But it is enough for now to consider only the way the mind distorts the images it receives.

Our ideas of the world would be very different if we could know it as it is, even in its observable, phenomenal aspect, instead of only through the vibrations modified by the mind. Direct and accurate knowing is by no means impossible, although it can be done only by those who have made great progress in controlling their minds. The vibrations of the mind can be stilled. An impact from without will then shape an image exactly corresponding to the source of the impact, the inner and outer vibrations being identical in quality and quantity, not intermixed with already present vibrations belonging to the observer. We can develop this process of mind control by techniques such as Raja Yoga, by which we can gain a true knowledge of things.

Reading maketh a full man, conference a ready man, and writing an exact man.
—Francis Bacon

Chapter Three

The truth is that we generally know only our impressions of things, not the actual things, and this truth is of vital importance in practical life. It teaches humility, caution, and readiness to listen to new ideas. If we realize this truth, we lose our instinctive certainty that we are right in our observations, and we learn to analyze ourselves before we reject the views of others.

An illustration may help to make this clearer. I meet someone whose vibratory activity expresses itself in a way opposite to my own. When we meet, we are not "in sync" with each other; hence we do not like each other. We do not see anything worthwhile in one another, and we each wonder why some people think the other is so clever. Now, if I have gained a little self-knowledge, I will check this aversion. Instead of thinking that other persons are stupid, I ask myself: "What is lacking in me that I cannot answer their vibrations sympathetically? If I cannot realize their life and thought, it is because I cannot reproduce their vibrations. Why should I judge them, since I cannot even know them until I modify myself sufficiently to be able to respond to them harmoniously?"

We cannot greatly modify others, but we can modify ourselves, and we should continually try to enlarge our own receptive capacity. We can try to become like the colorless light, in which all colors are present; it distorts none because it rejects none. It has in itself the power to reveal each accurately. Our power of response to the most diverse characters is a measure of our approach to all-inclusiveness. The essential self in us is all-inclusive because it is ultimately the One Self, in which all are latent possibilities.

THE BUILDING AND EVOLUTION OF THE MENTAL BODY

We need to understand clearly how consciousness builds up the mind as its vehicle because every day and hour of our lives provide opportunities for applying our minds in important ways. Waking or sleeping, we are constantly building our mental bodies; for whenever consciousness vibrates, it affects the mind stuff surrounding it. That mind stuff is composed of particles of mental matter, just as physical stuff is composed of physical particles. Every quiver of consciousness, even from a passing thought, draws some particles of mind stuff into the mental body, and shakes out other particles from it.

Vibration in the mental body depends on our being pulled or pushed—attracted or repelled—by things. This alternating motion is caused by the consciousness reacting to something in the not-self. When it is attracted, the mind reproduces in itself the vibrations of the attractive thing and so becomes like it. When it is repelled, the mind reasserts its identity by rejecting the not-self's vibrations and reinforcing its own. In either case, the matter in the mental body is thus thrown into waves, as is the mental matter in the field surrounding that body, which serves as a medium for affecting the consciousness of others.

The fineness or coarseness of the mental matter thus stirred to vibration depends on the quality of those vibrations. "High" thoughts are rapid vibrations that can affect only the subtle grades of mind stuff. The denser grades remain unaffected, being unable to vibrate at the necessary speed. When a lofty thought causes the mental body to vibrate, particles of the denser matter are shaken out, particles of the finer grades take their place, and better materials are built into the mental body. Similarly, sensually crass or emotionally disturbing thoughts draw into the mental body the coarser materials suitable for their own expression, and these materials repel and drive out finer kinds.

In this way, vibrations of consciousness are always shaking out one kind of matter and building in another. It follows, inevitably, that the kinds of matter we have built into our mental bodies in the past affect our power of responding to the thoughts that now reach us from outside. If our mental bodies are composed of finer materials, coarse thoughts meet with no response and hence inflict no injury; whereas if our mental bodies have been built up with coarse materials, they are affected by every coarse thought around us and remain unresponsive to elevated thoughts.

When we come into touch with persons who regularly think "high" thoughts, their thought vibrations, playing on us, arouse vibrations of any matter in our mental bodies that is capable of responding. The benefit we receive from such people is thus largely dependent on our own past thinking; and our ability to understand and respond to their thoughts is largely conditioned by our own past thoughts. Other persons can affect our consciousness only by stimulating vibrations in our mental bodies that are similar to their own.

However, understanding (that is, the ability to respond appropriately with harmonious vibrations of our own) does not always immediately follow the production of such vibrations from outside. Sometimes the effect resembles that of the sun, the rain, and the earth on the seed that lies buried in the ground. At first there is no visible answer to the vibrations playing on the seed; but within there is a tiny quiver of the ensouling life. That quiver grows stronger and stronger day by day, until the evolving life bursts the seed's shell and sends forth a rootlet and a growing sprout. So it is with the mind. The consciousness only slowly develops understanding, which is the ability to respond appropriately to the external impacts on it.

Similarly, before we are capable of fully understanding a thought by vibrating harmoniously with it, we may experience a partial understanding, an unconscious quivering that is the forerunner of a conscious response. When we leave the presence of a great thinker, we remain a little nearer to the rich thought life flowing from that person. Seeds of thought have been quickened in us, and our minds have been helped in their development.

Some part, then, of the building and evolution of our minds may be done from outside, but most of the change must come from the activities of our own consciousness. If we want to have strong, well vitalized, active mental bodies, able to grasp the "lofty" thoughts we encounter, then we must steadily work at thinking well; for we are our own builders and fashion our minds for ourselves.

Chapter Three

BUILDING THE POWER OF THOUGHT

Many people are great readers, but reading alone does not build the mind; thought is what builds it. Reading is valuable only for furnishing materials for thought. We may read much, but our mental growth will be in proportion to the amount of thinking we do along with the reading. "Reading makes a full man," said Francis Bacon, the Renaissance philosopher. As eating fills the stomach, reading fills the mind. But both food and reading matter must be digested before they can nourish body and mind. The mind does not grow by passive absorption; instead, it is likely to suffer from overloading and to become weaker rather than stronger under a burden of unassimilated ideas.

Many people read quickly for a while, and then put the book away until the next time for reading comes. In that way, their power of thought grows only very slowly. We should read less and think more if we want our minds to grow and our intelligence to develop. If we are in earnest about expanding our minds, we should spend an hour a day studying some serious and important material by reading for five minutes and thinking for ten throughout the hour.

Those who are eager to grow should make a resolution that no day will pass without at least twice as much intense thinking as reading. At first they may find the effort laborious and so discover the weakness of their thinking power. The discovery that one is unable to think hard and consecutively is the first step toward growth, for people who cannot think, but who think that they can, do not make much progress. It is better to know one's weakness than to imagine oneself strong when one is actually feeble.

The wandering of our mind or the feeling of confusion and fatigue that comes over our brain after prolonged effort to follow a difficult line of thought is similar to the weary feeling in our muscles after strong physical exertion. With regular and persistent but not excessive exercise, thought power grows as muscle power grows. And as this thought power grows, it also comes under control and can be directed to particular ends. Without such controlled thinking, the mental body will remain loosely formed and unorganized. Without concentrating thought on a definite point, we cannot exercise thought power at all.

APPLICATIONS

1. The next time you are with someone you do not resonate with, regard that person very carefully. Don't judge, observe. And look for qualities in that person that you yourself could benefit from developing.

2. Choose a page from a challenging book. First read the page quickly and list the ideas you remember from it. Then read the page slowly and thoughtfully, pausing frequently to contemplate what it says. Look at the list you made earlier and add any new ideas you have noticed. Also add notes about the ideas that came to you from contemplating what you read. When might the first procedure be appropriate? When the second?

A thought comes when it will, not when I will.
—William James

There are two distinct classes of what are called thoughts: those that we produce in ourselves by reflection and the act of thinking, and those that bolt into the mind of their own accord.
—Thomas Paine

For provocation of thought, we use ourselves and use each other. Some perceptions—I think the best—are granted to the single soul; they come from the depth and go to the depth and are the permanent and controlling ones. Others it takes two to find. We must be warmed by the fire of sympathy, to be brought into the right conditions and angles of vision.
—Ralph Waldo Emerson

Chapter Four

THOUGHT TRANSFERENCE

CHAPTER SUMMARY

Thought transference, although going on constantly all around us, is largely unconscious and undirected.

Thought transference happens in either of two ways. One is from brain to brain by way of the subtle, etheric levels of physical reality. The other is from mind to mind through the mental atmosphere all around us.

The mental atmosphere created by all of us collectively forms public opinion and national habits of thought and prejudices.

Despite all these influences on us, we each have the power to control whatever thoughts come to us and to decide how to respond to them.

ALMOST EVERYONE nowadays is aware of the possibility of thought transference or telepathy, of communicating with an absent friend without using a physical medium like telephone, postal mail, or e-mail. Dr. J. B. Rhine, a psychologist at Duke University, conducted experiments from 1930 onward into extrasensory perception and telepathy that found positive results beyond the chance level. His are the most famous experiments, but there are also more recent ones with even more convincing results. Some people think that they can transfer thought with very little effort, and are quite surprised when they discover they cannot. Yet it is clear that we must be able to think clearly and steadily before we can send a thought to someone else.

Feeble, vacillating thoughts cause only flickering vibrations in the thought atmosphere, appearing and vanishing moment by moment, giving rise to vague forms with little energy. A thought form must be clearly defined and well energized if we are to send it in any particular direction, and it must be strong enough, on arriving at its destination or "target," to set up a reproduction of itself there.

There are two methods of thought transference, one that is physical, the other psychical; one belongs to the brain as well as the mind, the other to the mind only. In the first method, a thought you have may cause vibrations in your mental body, next in your astral body, then in etheric matter, and from there in the dense molecules of your physical brain. At the same time, these vibrations, which are in both your dense physical brain and its subtler etheric counterpart, pass outward in the subtle or etheric matter of the physical world, until they reach another person's brain and set up vibrations in both its etheric and dense parts. The brain that receives the vibrations passes them on to the receiver's emotional and mental bodies, and those vibrations in the mental body draw out a response in that person's consciousness. Such are the many stages of the arc traversed by a thought.

However, this traversing of a loop from mind to brain to another brain and mind is not necessary. The consciousness may, when causing vibrations in its mental body, send those vibrations directly to the mental body of another receiving consciousness, thus avoiding the loop just described. This is the second and more direct method of thought transference.

BRAIN-TO-BRAIN TRANSFERENCE

Let us see what happens in the first case. There is a small organ in the brain, the pineal gland, the function of which is to secrete the hormone melatonin, which affects skin color and is related to our circadian biorhythms. The French philosopher René Descartes, however, thought it was the seat of the soul, and H. P. Blavatsky associated it with spiritual consciousness. It seems to be a rudimentary organ in most people, but some clairvoyants have seen it as evolving, rather than atavistic. They report that it is possible to quicken its evolution so that it can perform a function that in the future will be active in everyone, for they say that the pineal gland is the organ of thought transference, as much as the eye is the organ of vision or the ear of hearing.

If we think very intently on a single idea with concentration and sustained attention, we may become conscious of a slight quiver or creeping feeling deep in the center of the brain. This quiver is said to be in the pineal gland, particularly in the etheric matter that permeates the gland, causing a mild current that gives rise to the feeling. If the thought is strong enough to cause the current, then we know that we have been successful in clearly defining the thought and energizing it enough to transmit it through subtle etheric matter.

The current thus generated in turn passes through the etheric matter between two brains and produces vibrations in the etheric matter of the pineal gland of the second brain. The waves are then transmitted to the emotional and mental bodies of the receiver, thus reaching that person's consciousness. If this second pineal gland cannot reproduce the vibrations, however, the thought will not have been transferred, just as waves of light make no impression on a blind eye.

No scientific evidence exists to support this particular explanation of brain-to-brain thought transference. So it must be regarded as a theory to account for one possible mechanism of that thought transference, the existence of which does have experimental support.

MIND-TO-MIND TRANSFERENCE

In the second method of thought transference, the thinker creates a thought form at the mental level and, bypassing the brain, sends it directly to another thinker's mind. The power to do this deliberately requires a far higher mental evolution than does the physical method of thought transference because the sender must be self-conscious on the mental plane.

However, we all exercise this power continually, but usually indirectly and unconsciously, since all our thinking causes vibrations in our mental body. Because these unconscious vibrations are propagated to other minds through the surrounding mind stuff, there is no reason to confine the expression "thought transference" to conscious and deliberate transmissions of a particular thought from one person to another. The occurrence of the same idea to several persons simultaneously is likely to be the result of such transference. We are all continually affecting each other by these waves of thought sent out without clear intent, and what is called public opinion is largely created in this way. The ideas thus disseminated may be inchoate and poorly organized, but widespread.

PUBLIC OPINION AND NATIONAL PREJUDICES

Most people think in a certain way, not because they have carefully considered a question and come to a conclusion, but because a large number of other people are thinking along the same lines, and mass opinion carries them along with it. The strong thought of a great thinker goes out into the thought atmosphere and is caught up by receptive and responsive minds that reproduce that thinker's vibrations. The thought wave, thus amplified as it echoes in the minds of many, affects still others who would have remained unresponsive to the original vibrations without the amplifying influence of the echoes. With the added force of these others, the waves become still stronger, affecting ever larger masses of people. Public opinion, once formed, exercises a dominant sway over the minds of the great majority as it beats unceasingly on all brains and causes responsive vibrations in them.

Certain national ways of thinking cut clear, deep channels. Those ways result from centuries of continual reproduction of similar thoughts that arise from the history, the struggles, and the customs of a nation. They profoundly modify and color all minds born into that nation, and everything that comes from outside the nation is changed by the national vibration rate. As our individual mental bodies modify thoughts that come to us from the outer world, so do nations modify impressions from other nations by their own national vibration rate. The result is a national personality and habit of mind.

As a result, people in different countries see the same facts, but add their own presuppositions and accuse each other of falsifying facts and practicing unfair methods. If this inevitable truth were recognized, international quarrels might be smoothed more easily, wars could be avoided, and those waged would be more easily ended. If each nation recognized the national bias inherent in the views of every country and, instead of blaming another nation for differences of opinion, sought to reconcile conflicting views, they could avoid a great deal of strife and achieve a more enduring peace.

When public opinion changes,
it is with the rapidity of thought.
—Thomas Jefferson

Thoughts may be bandits. Thoughts may be raiders. Thoughts may be invaders. Thoughts may be disturbers of the international peace.
—Woodrow Wilson

LIVING IN THE ATMOSPHERE
OF MIXED THOUGHT

A very practical question for each of us arises from the knowledge of this continual and general thought transference. We live inevitably in a mixed atmosphere, in which helpful and harmful thought vibrations are constantly active and are insinuated into our consciousness. How can we guard ourselves against injurious thought transference, and how can we benefit from that which is helpful? To answer that question, we need to know how to select certain influences and avoid others.

Each of us influences our own mental body constantly, while others influence it only occasionally. The speaker to whom we listen or the author whose book we read influences our mental body only sporadically: we are the permanent factor. Our own influence over the composition of our mental body is far stronger than is that of anyone else, and we ourselves fix the normal vibration rate of our minds. We are responsible for what we are.

Thoughts that do not harmonize with our habitual rate will be flung aside when they touch the mind. If we think truth, a lie cannot lodge in our minds; if we think love, hate cannot disturb us; if we think wisdom, ignorance cannot paralyze us. Here alone is safety from unwanted influence, here is real power over ourselves. We must not allow our mind to lie fallow, for then any thought seed may take root and grow; we must not remain passive and allow our mind to vibrate randomly, for it may then respond to any passing vibration.

Here lies the practical lesson. If we put this lesson into practice, we will soon find its value and discover that, by using our power of thought, we can make our

49

lives nobler and happier and that, by the wisdom that comes from wise thought, we can put an end to pain.

APPLICATIONS

1. People vary greatly in their ability to send and receive thoughts by direct transference. The psychologist J. B. Rhine tested this ability with what are called "Zener cards," a deck of 25 cards, consisting of five designs, each repeated five times: cross, star, circle, wave, rectangle. One way of using the cards is for a sender to shuffle the deck and then look at the cards one at a time, forming a mental image of the design on each card as it is turned up. A receiver tries to tune into the sender's mind and writes down the design that suggests itself. The sender and receiver should not be in direct physical contact with each other, but a signal, such as a knock or bell, can be used to indicate when it is time to move to the next card. You can make a deck of Zener cards from 25 three-by-five filing cards by drawing the designs on one side of each. An average or chance rate is 5 correct guesses for one pass through the whole deck. Many factors affect this sort of thought transference, but you might find it interesting to try.

2. Here is another sort of experiment: Every time a negative thought enters your mind, immediately call to mind a corresponding positive thought in its place. Do this conscientiously for a week and then evaluate the effect of the practice on yourself.

3. Find examples of strong red, yellow, and blue colors. You and a partner both gaze at these colors. Then both close your eyes. You as sender visualize one of the colors and send the thought of it to your partner, who tells you which color came to mind. After several tries, change roles. Keep a record of hits and misses. A score of 33 percent correct would be expected by chance. This experiment can also be done in groups, with two or more people together sending to a group of two or more.

4. When you hear the telephone ring, before you answer it, note your impression of who is calling. Keep a record of your hits and misses. If you have access to the *Journal of the Society for Psychical Research*, read Rupert Sheldrakes's article in the October 2000 issue on "Telepathic Telephone Calls."

*All thinking is . . . a state of unrest
tending towards equilibrium.*
—Samuel Butler

*Mere experience can as little as reading
supply the place of thought. Experience stands
to thinking in the same relation in which eating
stands to digestion and assimilation.*
—Arthur Schopenhauer

*Thinking is the combining of two or
more ideas to embody another idea.*
—Ernest Wood

Chapter Five

THE BEGINNINGS
OF THOUGHT

CHAPTER SUMMARY

We come into the world with our minds already partially stocked with certain general ideas we have inherited from our evolutionary past, as a species and as individuals.

Stimuli produce sensations that the knowing self responds to by linking various sensations together as the perception of an object.

Thinking is our ability, as the knower, to link together sensations stimulated through various senses and to relate them to the external world and to ourselves.

Thought is not a sequence of isolated processes, but a whole involving physical stimuli, sensations of pleasure and pain, desire or aversion aroused by the stimuli, innate conceptual categories, the ability to associate, and a consciousness to be aware of all this.

Chapter Five

*All thought is a feat of association: having
what's in front of you bring up something in your
mind that you almost didn't know you knew.
Putting this and that together. That click.*
—Robert Frost

F EW PERSONS outside the circle of students of psychology have troubled themselves much with the question of how thought originates. Furthermore, even psychologists are not able to study by direct observation the beginnings of thought, for when we come into the world, we find ourselves possessing (or being possessed by) a large amount of ready-made thought, a store of what are sometimes called "innate ideas." These are general ideas we bring with us into the world, the condensed or summarized results of our collective evolution as a species and our personal experiences in previous lives.

Philosophers like Immanuel Kant, psychotherapists like Carl G. Jung, and linguists like Noam Chomsky all recognize that we have innate mental structures, although they talk about those structures in very different ways. However we talk about these structures, we begin our transactions in this life with such mental stock-in-hand.

Psychologists can, however, learn something about the origin of thought by observing infants. Just as the new physical body is said to recapitulate in prenatal life the long physical evolution of the past, according to the principle that ontogeny (the development of the individual) recapitulates phylogeny (the development of the species), so does a new mental body swiftly traverse the stages of the long evolution of human mentality. However, the "mental body" is not by any means identical with "thought," and so even in studying an infant's use of its new mental body, we are not really studying the "beginnings of thought." Moreover, using ordinary means, we cannot study the mental body directly, but only through its effects on the physical brain and nervous system.

Thought is as distinct from the mental body as it is from the physical; it pertains to consciousness, to the life side, whereas the mental and physical bodies both belong to the form or matter side as transitory vehicles or instruments. As already said, we should always keep before us the distinction between ourselves as a knower and the mental body, which is our instrument for obtaining knowledge.

However, by observing the effects of thought on a mental body when it is new, we can infer by analogy something of the beginnings of thought when a self first comes into contact with the not-self. The observations can help us because of the principle stated in the axiom "as above, so below." That is, everything we observe reflects other parallel or analogous things, and by studying the reflections, we can learn something of their parallels and analogs.

SENSATIONS, PERCEPTIONS, AND THE SELF

If we observe an infant closely, we see that sensations—responses to stimuli by feelings of pleasure or pain, and especially the latter—precede any sign of self-awareness or intelligence; vague sensations precede definite cognitions. Before birth, the infant was sustained by the life forces flowing through the mother's body. When the infant is launched on an independent existence, the direct maternal life forces are cut off. As the mother's life forces lessen, the infant feels want, and this want is pain. Gratification of the want brings pleasure, and the infant sinks back into unconsciousness. A little later, sights and sounds evoke a response, but still no sign of self-aware intelligence is apparent.

The first sign of intelligence is when the sight or voice of the mother is connected with the satisfaction of the ever-recurring want, with the giving of pleasure by food. A group of recurring sensations are linked together in or by memory and become associated with one external object, the "mother." The infant recognizes this object as separate from its sensations, but the cause of their satisfaction. Thought is the cognition of a relation between a group of sensations and one object that links them together. This is the first expression of intelligence, a rudimentary thought called a "perception." The essence of this process is establishing a relation between a unit of consciousness—a self—and an object, linking the self with not-self. Wherever such a relation is established, thought is present.

This simple fact can serve as a general example of the beginning of thought in a separated self encased in its five envelopes of matter, however fine that matter is. In such a separated self, sensations precede thoughts; the attention of the self is aroused through an impression made by a sensation that it responds to. A feeling of want does not itself arouse thought. But that want, satisfied in an infant by its contact with milk, creates an impression, followed by a feeling of pleasure.

After this process has been repeated often enough, the self, vaguely and gropingly, reaches outward in the direction from which the impression came. At the same time, the life energy flows into the mental body and energizes it, so that it reflects, faintly at first, the object that has caused the sensation. This modification in the mental body, repeated time after time, stimulates the self in its aspect of knowledge, and the self vibrates correspondingly. Want, contact, and pleasure have been felt, and with the contact an image presents itself. Sight and taste are both involved, and the two sense impressions blend. The inherent nature of the self as knower links these three— the want, the contact image, and the pleasure—and this link is incipient thought.

SENSATION AND THOUGHT

It is widely recognized in psychology, Eastern and Western, that all thought is rooted in sensation, that there can be no thinking until a large number of sensations have been accumulated. "Mind, as we know it," says H. P. Blavatsky (*Secret Doctrine* 1:2n), "is resolvable into states of consciousness, of varying duration, intensity, complexity, etc.,—all, in the ultimate, resting on sensation."

Many spiritual teachings, East and West, tell us that we shape ourselves and our world with our thoughts.
—Frances Vaughan

Some writers have gone farther than this, declaring that not only are sensations the materials out of which thoughts are constructed, but that thoughts are produced by sensations alone, thus ignoring any thinker, any knower. Others, at the opposite extreme, maintain that thought is solely the result of the activity of the thinker, apart from any sensations. In this latter view, thought arises from within instead of receiving its first impulse from without, and sensations are only the materials the thinker uses, not a necessary condition for thought.

Each of those two views contains part of the truth, but the full truth lies between them. It is necessary for the awakening of the knower that sensations coming from outside should play upon consciousness. The first thought arises in consequence of impulses from sensation. Yet without an inherent capacity for linking things together and a capacity for knowledge, the self might experience a stream of random sensations without ever producing a thought, as in the case of an autistic child. It is only half the truth that thoughts have their beginning in sensations. An organizing and relating power must work on those sensations to link them to one another and to the external world. The thinker and the sensation combine to generate thought as their child.

If thoughts have their beginnings in sensations, and those sensations are caused by vibrational impacts from outside, then it is most important to observe accurately the nature and extent of sensation. It is well known that an environment rich in interesting sensory stimuli helps a baby to develop intelligence.

The first work of the knower is to observe; if there were nothing to observe, the knower would remain forever asleep. But when an object is presented and the self is conscious of an impact, then the knower observes. The accuracy of that observation determines the thought shaped by it and others linked with it. If the observation is inaccurate, if a mistaken relation between the object and the knower is established, then out of that error will grow a number of consequent errors that nothing can put right except going back to the very beginning and starting over.

Consider a particular case of sensation and perception. Suppose I sense a touch on my hand. When I sense a touch, I just sense—nothing more need be added as far as that pure sensation is concerned. But when I pass from the sensing to the object that caused the sensation, I perceive that object, and this perception is a thought. The perception means that I as knower recognize a relationship between myself and the object that caused the sensation.

This recognition, however, is not all that happens. I also experience other sensations: color, form, softness, warmth, texture. These are again passed on to me as knower, and, aided by the memory of similar impressions received earlier—that is, by comparing past images with the image of the object touching the hand—I decide on the kind of object that has touched it.

Thought and feeling take counsel together and supplement one another in turn.
—Vauvenargues

59

Chapter Five

THE HOLISM OF THOUGHT

The beginning of thought lies in the perception of what has caused a sensation. That is, the beginning of cognition is the perception of a not-self as the cause of certain sensations experienced by the self. Feeling by itself, if that were possible, could not give rise to consciousness of the not-self; the self would have only the feeling of pleasure or pain, an inner consciousness of expansion or contraction. No higher human evolution would be possible if we could do nothing more than feel. Only when we recognize objects as causes of pleasure or pain does human cognition begin. All mental evolution depends on establishing a conscious relation between the self and the not-self. That evolution largely consists of these relations becoming more and more numerous, more and more complicated, and more and more accurately made by the knower. The knower begins to unfold when the awakened consciousness, feeling pleasure or pain, looks on the external world and says, "That object gave me pleasure; that object gave me pain."

The self must have experienced a large number of sensations before responding externally at all. Eventually the willing self begins a dull, confused groping after a pleasure because it desires to repeat it. Thinking and feeling are intimately related, for the desire to repeat a pleasure implies that the picture of the pleasure remains in consciousness, however faintly. This picture is memory and is an aspect of thought.

For a long time in infancy, the half-awakened self drifts from one thing to another, striking against the not-self in haphazard fashion, without direction. The self experiences pleasure and pain without perceiving the cause of either. Only when this has gone on for a long time is the perception mentioned above possible, and then the relation between the knower and the known begins.

APPLICATIONS

1. Take an object, such as an orange or any other handy object. Note the stimuli that come from it through your various senses (color, texture, scent, flavor, sound when tapped or segmented). Note the sensations that those stimuli produce (how you feel about the stimuli). Note how the perception of "an orange" arises from the linking together of those stimuli and sensations. The next is harder. Which, if any, aspects of your perception of "an orange" might have come, not from your experience of stimuli and sensations, but from ideas innate in your mind? Is there anything about the orange that you have not learned from past experience?

2. When you are awakened in the night by an unidentified sound, observe your mind's trying to identify it. You may glimpse the relationship between sensation and thought.

Memory is the power to gather roses in winter.
—Anonymous

Think of three Things: whence you came, where you are going, and to whom you must account.
—Benjamin Franklin

Imagination and memory are but one thing, which for divers considerations hath divers names.
—Thomas Hobbes

Chapter Six

THE NATURE OF MEMORY

CHAPTER SUMMARY

Patterns tend to repeat themselves. The repetition of mental patterns, of vibrations in the mental body, is the basis of memory.

Vibrations in any form of matter anywhere in the world are repeated continuously in subtler forms of matter, and that repetition is the memory of nature, also called the akashic records.

Good memory is a matter of interest, attention, accurate observation, and clear thinking. It is motivated either by our attraction to external objects or by the will, based on our judgment of the value of the objects. We can improve our memory by the regular practice of observing, forming mental images, and making associations.

Memory is the contemplation and association of images originally experienced in the past; anticipation is the contemplation and association of images projected into the future.

Chapter Six

The good man is glad to hold converse with himself, for he has pleasant memories of the past and fair hopes for the future, on which he can dwell with satisfaction; nor has he any lack of topics upon which to exercise the speculative powers of his mind.

—Aristotle

WE ALL WANT to experience pleasure and avoid pain. Once we have associated some object with pleasure, we want to contact that object again and so repeat the pleasure. On the other hand, once we have associated an object with pain, we avoid that object to escape the pain. If we find pleasure in the taste of chocolate, we eat chocolate; if we find displeasure in the taste of castor oil, we avoid castor oil. That is obvious. But the same principle applies in our thinking.

Once an association has been made in our minds between some thing and either pleasure or pain, that association gets strengthened by repetition, and it flows both ways. If for whatever reason we begin to think about pleasant or unpleasant tastes, our mind reproduces an image of the object associated with that pleasure or displeasure—a chocolate bar or a teaspoon of castor oil. This association works because of the general principle that energy flows in the direction of least resistance, in this case, a reshaping of the matter of the mental body into forms it has already taken. Whatever we have done in the past, we tend to do again. The mental body's tendency to repeat earlier vibrations is due to the tendency of matter to stay in the same state (inertia), and this tendency is the seed of memory.

Molecules of matter that have been grouped together by some force slowly fall apart as other energies play on them. But for a considerable time they retain a tendency to resume their mutual relation. If they are subjected to an impulse like one that grouped them earlier, they quickly fall again into their former position. Similarly, when the knower has once vibrated in any particular way, that pattern of vibration is likely to recur. In the case of an object that gives pleasure or pain, the desire for the object or for avoiding it stimulates the mental body to repeat the pattern of the vibration associated with the object, thereby reproducing an image of it.

The image thus produced is recognized by the knower and, in the case of attachment caused by pleasure, stimulates the reproduction of the image of the pleasure. The repulsion caused by pain equally brings up the image of the pain. Experience has connected the object with pleasure or pain. Activating the set of vibrations that compose the image of the object stirs up the set of vibrations that make up the pleasure or the pain. Thus the pleasure or the pain is experienced again, even though the object is not present.

This is memory in its simplest form: pleasure or pain re-experienced by a self-initiated vibration of earlier feelings. These remembered images are less prominent or "lighter"—and hence to the partially developed knower less vivid—than those caused by direct contact with an external object. Vibrations from such direct contact by the physical senses are more prominent and "heavier," so they generate more energy in the images they produce.

Yet sense-caused vibrations and memory-caused ones are basically the same sort of vibrations, for memory is the reproduction in mental matter of objects the knower has previously contacted.

Memory is not limited to a single individual. There are shared memories also: family memories, community memories, national memories, and memories that are common to our whole species. C. G. Jung called the last our "collective unconscious." A collective memory is made up from the memories of the individual members of a group. So a family memory is based on the shared memories of all the family members, but it acquires a life of its own apart from the individual members.

But shared memories do not stop with our species. Our whole planet has a memory, the "Gaia memory" we might call it. And beyond that there is even a universal memory, the memory of the cosmos, which is sometimes called the "akashic records," using a term from Sanskrit, *akasha*, that means "space." The universal memory is made up from the memories of all the beings in the universe, but has a life of its own as well. If we ask how that universal memory comes into existence, we may think of an analogy.

If we shine a flashlight into the night sky, its light travels outward into the heavens. The farther it goes, the weaker it becomes, but in principle it continues to shine to the farthest reaches of the universe. The stars and galaxies throughout the universe are like gigantic flashlights; they are so powerful that we can see their light across immense expanses of space and through eons of time.

Our individual thoughts and memories are something like the light from a flashlight, and our collective thought and memory is something like the light from a star. But thoughts and memories do not travel through physical space. Instead they travel through the "space" of *akasha*, which contains the various "planes" of nature: dense physical, etheric, emotional, mental, causal, and still other more subtle planes. In *akasha* no thoughts or memories are ever lost; they are always available to be recovered from this cosmic memory, which is the memory of the Logos or Intelligence of the Universe, and they last as long as the universe does.

On the cosmic scale, the reflection of objects that begins in an individual's mind is repeated over and over, in the ever subtler matter of one plane after another, without regard to the individual knower. These reflected images in their totality are the partial contents of the memory of the Logos, the Intelligence of a Universe. Any individual separated self may contact these images according to that knower's ability to harmonize with the appropriate vibrations. In radio or television, a series of vibrations (electromagnetic waves) can be caught by any receiver capable of translating them into sound and picture. So these cosmic images of a particular vibration can activate a similar latent vibratory potency within a knower.

Thought runs ahead and foresees outcomes, and thereby avoids having to await the instruction of actual failure and disaster.
—John Dewey

Chapter Six

Bad Memory

To understand what lies at the root of "bad memory," we must examine in more detail the mental processes that make up memory. Many factors influence what we remember. We tend to remember longest things we encounter frequently, but we recall best in the short term things encountered first and most recently, things that are unusual or unexpected, things that are specific and can be visualized, things that relate to one another or are associated with other things already familiar to us, and so on. Memory is a complex phenomenon.

Although memory is often spoken of as a single mental faculty, there is really no one faculty to which that name can be given. The persistence of a mental image depends on the general quality of the mind. A feeble mind holds an image feebly. Like a substance too fluid to retain the shape of the mold from which it has been poured, such a mind falls quickly out of the form it has taken. If the mental body is poorly organized—is a mere loose aggregate of the molecules of mind stuff like a mass of clouds without much coherence—memory will certainly be weak. But this weakness is general, not specific; it is common to the whole mind and is due to its low stage of development.

As the mental body becomes better organized and the powers of the self work in it, we still often find inaccurate or incomplete memory. But if we observe this latter "bad memory," we find that it is not faulty in all respects; there are some things that are remembered well and that the mind retains without effort. If we examine these remembered things, we find that they greatly attract the person's mind; things that a person likes are not forgotten. A person may complain of a bad memory with respect to a subject he has to study, but still have a very retentive memory for the details of a sport he is interested in. His mental body is not lacking in a fair amount of retentiveness. When he observes carefully and attentively, producing a clear mental image, the image is long-lived.

Here we have a key to "bad memory." It is due to lack of interest, which causes lack of accurate observation, and therefore leads to confused thought. Confused thought is the blurred impression caused by careless observation and lack of attention, whereas clear thought is the sharply cut impression due to concentrated attention and careful, accurate observation. We do not remember the things to which we pay little attention, but we remember well the things that keenly interest us.

How, then, should a "bad memory" be treated? First, we should notice which things we remember and which we forget. Then we should scrutinize the things we forget, in order to see if they are worth remembering. If we find that we care very little about them, but that we believe we ought to care about them, then we should say to ourselves, "I will pay attention to them, observe them accurately, and think carefully and steadily on them." If we do this, our memory will improve. The element of attraction is valuable in fixing our attention, but if it is not present, its place may be taken by an act of will.

It is exactly here that a difficulty arises. What moves the will? How can the will take the place of attraction? Attraction arouses desire, and desire impels us to move toward the attractive object. When an impulse to action is motivated by external objects and so is *drawn* forth, we call that impulse desire. When it is motivated by reason and judgment and is *sent* forth, we call it will. What is needed, then, in the absence of an attraction we feel to something outside ourselves is an intention produced inside ourselves.

Consider an example. Suppose we feel we should study a difficult subject. That study will need hours of concentration, which will be fatiguing, strenuous, and without much pleasure. The study does not attract us as an object of desire. Yet we understand that knowledge gained from this study will be the foundation on which we can build a deeper understanding of life, and that it will lead to our becoming wiser and thus better able to be of service to others. Our reason and judgment tell us that our good, as well as the good of others, will be served by the effort we put into the study. Thus we gain a motive by intellectually surveying the field and exercising judgment about the highest good; what the reason selects as leading to good serves as a motive for the will.

Once we have aroused the will in this way, then in moments of lassitude or weakness, we can stimulate the will again by recalling the train of thought that led to the choice in the first place. What we have deliberately chosen will seem attractive and desirable if we picture its pleasing qualities and its potential for giving happiness to ourselves or others.

The memory strengthens as you lay burdens upon it, and becomes trustworthy as you trust it.
—Thomas de Quincey

If we will to have something, we can also will to have the means of attaining it. We can overcome the natural shrinking from effort and unpleasant discipline by a will that is motivated by reason. In the example of studying a difficult subject, having determined that learning and wisdom are desirable because they lead to happiness, we use our will to carry out the activities that lead to attaining them.

In cultivating the power of observation, as in everything else, a little practice repeated daily is much more effective than a great effort followed by a period of inaction. We should set ourselves the daily task of observing carefully. If we give five minutes a day to practicing observation, we can rapidly improve our memory. Improving our powers of observation involves attention, imagination, and concentration. In doing so, we are organizing the mental body and preparing it to carry out its functions effectively. If we practice observation regularly, we will soon see that our powers have increased and have come much more under the control of our will.

Another way to improve our memory is to present things to our mind in an attractive form or associate them with attractive things. If we are visually oriented, we can improve a bad memory by constructing a picture and attaching the things we want to remember to points in that picture. Calling up the picture then also brings up the things to be remembered. Or if we are auditorily oriented, we can remember through the jingle of a rhyme by weaving a series of dates or other facts into verses that stick in our mind. But far better than any of these ways is the rational method detailed above, by the use of which the mental body becomes better organized and more coherent in its content.

Chapter Six

MEMORY AND ANTICIPATION

Let us return to the undeveloped knower. When memory begins to function, anticipation quickly follows, because anticipation is memory projected into the future. When in memory we retaste a pleasure experienced in the past, desire seeks to regain the object that gave us the pleasure. When this retasting is thought of as the result of again experiencing that object in the outer world and enjoying it, we have anticipation. The knower dwells on the images of the object and of the pleasure connected with them. If to this we add the element of time—past and future—then contemplating whatever was enjoyed in the past is memory, and contemplating future enjoyment is anticipation.

In the *Yoga Sutras*, the legendary sage Patanjali says that for the practice of Yoga one must stop the "modifications of the thinking principle." The modifications he is talking about are uncontrolled, compulsive memory and anticipation. Every contact with the not-self modifies the mental body, rearranging part of the stuff of which that body is composed into a picture or image of the external object. As the last chapter noted, establishing relations between such images is thinking, as seen on the form side. Or correspondingly, modifications in the consciousness of the knower are thinking, as seen on the life side.

The pictures in the mental body very much resemble the impressions made by light waves on a film, forming images of the objects to which the film has been exposed. So on the "film" of the mental body, some of the matter of which it is composed is rearranged as a picture of the objects it has contacted as their vibrations impinge on it. The knower perceives these pictures, muses upon them, and after a while begins to arrange them and to modify them by responding vibrations. Because, as mentioned before, energy follows the line of least resistance, the same images are re-formed over and over again, making images of images. This process of reproducing images, with the addition of the time element, is memory and anticipation.

Concrete thinking is only a repetition in subtler matter of everyday experiences in dense matter, with this difference: the knower can stop and change the sequence, repeat the images, and hurry or slow them at will. We can delay an image and brood over it. We can learn a great deal by reexamining experiences at our leisure and thus recognize much that escaped us when we originally passed through those experiences.

Time, as we experience it collectively, is an awareness by the Logos, the Intelligence of our universe, of successive stages in the duration of the world. We, as the knower, can make our own time within our own private world, and we often do that, so time for us runs fast or slow, depending on the circumstances of our life. However, we cannot escape from our sense of linear time and succession and instead perceive duration as a whole—the eternal now—until we are able to touch the consciousness of the Logos, freeing ourselves from the material limitations of this world.

Everyone complains of his lack of memory
but no one of his lack of judgment.
—La Rochefoucauld

APPLICATIONS

1. Choose an object that appeals to you, either natural or manufactured, and examine it with care and in detail for five minutes, forming a mental image of it. Then put it aside or turn away from it. Let twenty-four hours pass, and then call up your mental image of the object. See how much and in what detail you can remember it. Give yourself several minutes to do that, and then look at the object itself again, to see how well you recalled it through your mental image of it. Again spend five minutes inspecting the object to see what you missed or misremembered. Put it aside again. Repeat this exercise with the same object every day for a week. The following week, choose a different object and repeat the experiment.

2. One way to remember things and their relationships is to associate them with a pattern or design.
This is a very old technique, used by Roman ora-
tors and many others. For this technique, you need
a basic layout that you know well, perhaps the
Kabbalistic Tree of Life, if you are familiar with it;
or the floor plan of a cathedral, with its crypt,
nave, choir, sanctuary, bell tower, and so on; or a
house with several floors and various rooms, each
decorated in a different style. When you have
something to remember, such as a speech or a
series of facts, connect bits of each part of the thing
to be remembered with specific areas of the layout. Envision yourself walking through the house
or cathedral or passing through the sefiroth of the
Kabbalistic tree. As you do so, you will encounter
the memorized bits associated with each area of
the layout as you come to them. This technique
works best for those with a good visual memory.

You can observe a lot by watching.
—Yogi Berra

Thinking is a brain exercise—and no faculty grows save as it is exercised.
—Elbert Hubbard

If the doors of perception were cleansed everything would appear to man as it is, infinite. For man has closed himself up 'til he sees all things through narrow chinks of his cavern.
—William Blake

Chapter Seven

THE GROWTH OF THOUGHT

CHAPTER SUMMARY

*Clear thinking requires both accurate observation and the
ability to receive impressions and retain them.*

*We typically pay attention only to those aspects of the world
around us that our past experience has conditioned
us to see; we need to expand our awareness to other
aspects, to observe more widely and more closely.*

*If we train our minds to observe automatically, we can later
call up images that we were not consciously aware of
at the time we first encountered them.*

*In addition to observing, thought requires associating, com-
paring, and differentiating our observations, and reasoning about them.*

*Mind training or education is not so much learning facts
as developing our ability to respond to and use facts.*

*Associating with those who are more developed than we
are, either in person or through their writings, is a way
of developing ourselves; we can learn from them, their
words, their minds, and their spirits.*

The thinker stands in the same relation to the ordinary book-philosopher as an eyewitness does to the historian; he speaks from direct knowledge of his own.
—Arthur Schopenhauer

CLEAR THINKING can be learned. We can all improve our minds because the capacity for intelligence and clear thought is an inherent human capacity that, like musical ability, can be enhanced by training. Accurate, clear thinking has two requirements. The first is attentive and accurate observation. The self as knower must observe the not-self with close attention and with a high degree of accuracy in order to reproduce faithfully within the mental body that not-self and thus unite with it as a known thing.

The second requirement is receptivity and tenacity in the mental body, the power of yielding quickly to impressions and of retaining them. The mental body must be developed enough to be sensitive to even the weaker vibrations of an external object—otherwise it cannot be modified into a perfect reproduction of that object. At first, the broad outline is all that is obtained, the details being blurred or even omitted. But as we evolve our faculties and build finer stuff into the mental body, we find that we receive from an external object much more than we did when we were less developed.

Our intellectual evolution is a process of increasing our ability to become aware of the world around us and to relate to it. Our spiritual evolution is a process of our coming to a greater realization of our essential oneness with all other living beings. Both of those processes require that we be able to think clearly. The progress of our evolution—the speed at which our latent intellectual and spiritual potencies become active powers—is thus in proportion to the attention and accuracy of our observation and the receptivity and tenacity of our mental body.

ATTENTIVE AND ACCURATE OBSERVATION

Suppose two groups of people are standing in a field watching a vivid sunset. One group consists of farm workers who observe nature primarily from the perspective of their livelihood. They look at the sky to see if it promises rain or sunshine. The second group consists of artists, painters let's say, trained to see and respond to various shades and tones of color from a purely esthetic point of view. All the vibrations caused by that vivid sunset are playing upon the several vehicles of consciousness of both groups, but they respond to them differently.

The farm workers see various colors in the sky and observe that there is a good deal of red, promising clear weather for the next day, good or bad for their crops, as the case may be. This is what they notice because it is what is important for them.

The painters are exposed to exactly the same light vibrations as those of the farm workers. But their image of the sunset is quite different. They observe the varying shades of color, hue melting into hue—translucent blue, rose, palest green lighted with golden gleams and flecked with royal purple because such differences are important to them.

Our hypothetical farm workers may also be conscious of the beauty of the scene, but their principal concern is its agricultural implications. Similarly, our hypothetical artists will know that the state of the sky presages weather conditions, but their attention is on the esthetic dimension of the sunset. The two groups are concerned with different aspects of reality, so they observe differently. The difference in the images evoked in the two groups does not lie outside them, but inside them, in the way they respond. It is the same sunset, but different people see it differently.

This example shows what is meant by the "evolution" of the knower. Each of us perceives only a part of the universe of action, beauty, and wisdom all around us, though its vibratory waves play on us from every side. Everything that is in the mind of the Logos of our world is playing on us and on our bodies at this moment. How much of it we can receive marks the stage of our evolution. What we need for growth is not to change the world around us, but to change ourselves—the self's ability to relate in manifold ways to the not-self. Everything is already available to us, but we have to develop our inherent capacity to receive it.

*A well-trained mind is made up, so to speak,
of all the minds of past ages: only a single mind
has been educated during all that time.*
—Bernard de Fontenelle

One element in clear thinking is accurate observation of all aspects of whatever we are observing. We have to begin our development of clear thinking on the dense physical plane, where our bodies come most strikingly into contact with the not-self. On this plane we touch the external world, and from there the vibrations pass inward—activating our latent inner powers.

CULTIVATING AUTOMATIC OBSERVATION

Accurate observation, then, is a faculty we need to cultivate. Most people go through the world with their eyes half-closed. We can each test our own skill in observing by asking ourselves, as we walk along a street, "What have I observed while on this street?" Some persons will have observed many things. Others will have observed only a few. Many will have observed next to nothing; no clear images will have been formed. The last may answer, "I was thinking of something else, and so did not observe the scene around me." If they were thinking of something more important than training the mental body and the power of attention by careful observation, they may have done well in their lack of observation. But if they were only dreaming or drifting aimlessly, then they wasted time that could have been better used by turning their attention and energy outward.

The famous illusionist Harry Houdini related that he trained his son to observe the contents of the stores he passed while walking along the streets of London. Eventually the child could name the typical contents of a store by merely throwing a glance at the store window as he passed by without stopping. Normal children are observant, and the intelligence they display is proportionate to their capacity of observing.

Developing the habit of observation is part of mind training. Those who practice such training will find that their minds become clearer, increase in power, and become more easily manageable, so that they can better direct their attention to any object they choose. This power of observation, once established, works automatically. Our mental bodies can automatically register images, which become available without special effort or attention if we need them later. Our attention does not need to be directed to objects within our range of conscious perception in order for our mental bodies to receive and preserve an impression of those objects.

A trivial but significant case of this kind happened to Annie Besant. While she was traveling in America, a question arose one day about the number on the engine of a train on which she and her companions had been traveling. The number instantly came into her mind. That experience was not, in any sense, a case of clairvoyance; if it had been clairvoyant perception, she would have had to hunt up the train mentally and look for its number. But without any conscious action on her part, her sense organs and mind had observed and registered the number as the train came into the station. When she needed the number, the mental image of the incoming train, with its number on the front of the engine, at once came into her awareness. This faculty of automatic memory, once established, is a useful one, for it means that although things passing around you did not attract your attention at the time, you can nonetheless recall them by looking at their record in your mental body.

This automatic activity of the mental body, outside the conscious activity of the self, goes on more extensively in all of us than might be supposed. For example, when subjects are hypnotized, they can report a number of detailed events that originally had not attracted their attention. These impressions had reached their mental body through their brain and had been impressed on both brain and mind. Consciousness fails to cognize many impressions that reach the mental body because it is normally alert enough to notice only the strongest ones. The others are usually overpowered by the far stronger conscious impressions. But in hypnotic trance, delirium, or dreams, the brain yields up its record of these automatic impressions. If the mind is trained to observe and record, then the consciousness can recover the earlier impressions whenever it wants them.

Thus, if two people walk down a street, one trained in observation and the other not, both receive a number of impressions of which neither is conscious at the time. But afterward the trained observer can recover those impressions, whereas the untrained observer cannot. The habit of clear, quick automatic observation is at the root of clear thinking. So those who want to develop thought power will do well to cultivate the habit of observation rather than drifting idly along wherever the stream of fancy may carry them.

Those whose thinking is confused are generally those who observe least accurately. There are exceptions, however. For example, persons whose intelligence is highly developed but habitually turned inward have mental bodies that have not been trained to respond to the outer world. Because they habitually engage in introspective thought, they are unobservant of passing objects and do not pay attention to what is going on in front of them. It may not be worth their while in this life to train their mental bodies to observe their surroundings automatically. They already have highly developed thought power, but of an introverted kind. They need to work at deliberate rather than automatic observation.

But how many unobservant people are really deeply engaged in thought? Many people are easily distracted by any thought image that happens to present itself to their minds, or they turn over the contents of their mind in an aimless way, much as a bored person goes through the pages of a magazine. Such activity is not thinking, for thinking means, as we have seen, the establishing of relations, the addition of new connecting links between thought images, which are vibrational patterns. In thinking, the knower deliberately and actively directs attention to these thought images and the connections between them.

The Evolution of Mental Faculties

As images accumulate, our work as knower becomes more complicated, and our activity with the images draws out one latent power after another. We no longer accept the external world merely as a source of objects that cause us pleasure or pain. Instead, we arrange the images side by side, study them in their various aspects, shift them about, and reconsider them.

We also begin to arrange our own observations. When one image brings up another, we observe the order of their succession. When a second has followed a first many times, we begin to look for the second when the first appears, and thus link the two together. This is our first attempt at logic. We reason that because A and B have always appeared successively, therefore when A appears, B will also soon appear. If our experience verifies this forecast, we link A and B together as "cause" and "effect." Many errors, however, are due to postulating a causal relationship too hastily.

Furthermore, through setting images side by side, we observe their likenesses and differences, and develop the power of comparison. We identify some images as plea-sure-giving, and search for them in the external world, developing judgment by the consequences of our choices. We evolve a sense of proportion, grouping objects togeth-er by their likenesses and separating them from others by their differences. Because at first we are easily misled by surface similarities, in this process also we make many errors, which have to be corrected by later observations.

So observation, discrimination, reason, compari-son, and judgment all develop together. These faculties increase with use, and the self as knower evolves by exer-cising them, by continually repeated action and reaction between the self and the not-self.

No one can be a great thinker who does not recognize that as a thinker it is his first duty to follow his intellect to whatever conclusions it may lead.
—John Stuart Mill

Chapter Seven

*Few people think more than two or three
times a year; I have made an international
reputation for myself by thinking once
or twice a week.*
—George Bernard Shaw

To speed up the evolution of these faculties, we need to exercise them deliberately and consciously, using the circumstances of daily life as opportunities. Just as we can train ourselves to observe in everyday life, so also we can accustom ourselves to see the points of likeness and difference in the objects around us, then draw conclusions and test those conclusions by further experience. If we compare and judge consciously and purposely, such deliberate exercise rapidly develops our latent power of thought into an active power we can use at will.

THE TRAINING OF THE MIND

To train the mind in any one direction is, to some extent, to train it in all directions, because any kind of mental training helps to organize the mind stuff of which the mental body is composed and increases its ability to respond. The increased ability can be directed to any end and is available for all purposes. A trained mind can be applied to a new subject and can grapple with it and master it in a way impossible for the untrained mind. Such training is one of the purposes of education.

Training the mind is not cramming it with facts, but drawing out its latent powers. The mind does not grow by being gorged with other people's thoughts, but by exercising its own faculties. It is said of the great Teachers who stand at the head of human evolution that they know everything that exists within the solar system. This does not mean that every fact in the world is always within their consciousness. It means instead that they have so well developed their inner ability to *know* that, whenever they turn their attention in any direction, they know the object to which it is turned.

This ability is much more useful than storing a large number of facts in the mind, just as it is more useful to see an object on which the eye is turned than to be blind and know it only through its description by others. The evolution of the mind is measured, not by the images it contains, but by the development of its inner capacity for knowing, the power to reproduce within itself anything that is presented. This power, once gained, is ours to use wherever and whenever we need it.

ASSOCIATION WITH GREAT THINKERS

The work of training the mind is greatly advanced by our coming into touch with those who are more highly evolved than we are, for they send out vibrations of a higher order than we are able to create. A piece of iron lying on the ground cannot start heat vibrations on its own; but if it happens to be placed near a fire, it responds to the heat vibrations of the fire and thus becomes hot. When we come near great thinkers, either in person or through reading their words, their vibrations play on our mental bodies and set up corresponding vibrations in us, so that we vibrate sympathetically with their thoughts.

Eager chess players want opponents who are more skilled than they are, so that they can learn by playing the game. A player can learn nothing from an unskilled opponent and not much from one whose skill is too greatly superior. In life, as in chess, we learn thinking ability from those whose skill is greater than ours, but not too much greater.

While we are in contact with great thinkers and thoughts, we may feel that our mental power has increased and that we grasp concepts that normally elude us. When we are not in direct touch with them or their thoughts, however, we may find that these concepts have become blurred and confused. We may listen to a lecture and more or less follow it. We go away satisfied, feeling that we have learned something. On the following day, wishing to share with a friend what we have learned, we find to our chagrin that we cannot reproduce the concepts that seemed so clear and luminous just the day before.

The great thinkers from whom we derive inspiration enjoyed insights beyond their own systems. They made statements hard to reconcile with the neat little ways of thought which we pin on to their names.
—Alfred North Whitehead

The sense that we know something we experienced earlier, but just cannot get hold of it, comes from our memory of older vibrations we experienced in the mental body. We are conscious of having realized the concepts, we remember the forms they took, and feel that, having once produced them, we should be able to reproduce them easily. But at the earlier time, it was the strong vibrations of the speaker or writer that shaped the forms in our mental body; those forms were molded from without, not from within.

Our inability to reproduce concepts we have heard means that we must repeatedly have help in shaping them before we have sufficient skill to reproduce them ourselves. The knower must have experienced such vibrations repeatedly before being able to reproduce them at will. By virtue of our own inherent nature, we can evolve the power to reproduce them after responding several times to their impact from outside ourselves. Our ability is brought out of latency by contact with a similar but already active power in another, and thus the stronger quickens the evolution of the weaker. This is one of the reasons for associating with persons more advanced than ourselves. We profit by contact with them and grow under their stimulating influence.

Though direct contact is the most effective channel for influence to pass from one person to another, a good deal can also be gained from wisely chosen books. In reading the work of a great writer, we should try for the time to maintain an open mind, so as to receive as many of the thought vibrations as possible.

When we have read the words, we should dwell on them, ponder over them, try to sense the thought they partially express, draw out of them all their hidden relationships. Our attention must be concentrated, so as to enter the mind of the writer through the veil of words. Such reading educates us and helps to advance our mental evolution. Less strenuous reading may serve as a pleasant pastime or store our minds with valuable facts, and so be useful. But receptive reading stimulates our evolution. It should not be neglected by those who seek to grow in order to serve.

To think is to search for clearings in a wood.
—Jules Renard

It belongs to the self-respect of intellect to pursue every tangle of thought to its final unravelment.
—Alfred North Whitehead

To look within and to seek without are the winter and summer, the day and night, the left and right foot of the soul's progress.
—Ernest Wood

In the effort to unfold our thought to a friend we make it clearer to ourselves.
—Ralph Waldo Emerson

APPLICATIONS

1. Take a walk on a busy street and be as alert as you can to everything going on around you—sights, sounds, odors, activities. When you finish the walk, call to mind as many specific observations as you can of what you witnessed. You can do this alone, or with others. In the latter case, by sharing your observations you can help one another to become more observant in the future, since each person is likely to have observed something the others did not.

2. Some puzzles ask you to pick out the differences between two pictures or to decide which two out of eight or so objects are the same. Such puzzles are not merely pastimes; they are good training in recognizing differences and similarities. Look for them in the comic pages of a newspaper, in magazines, or in puzzle books and spend a bit of time working them.

3. Everyday, arrange to spend some time in the company of someone whose mental abilities and thought powers are greater than yours. That company may be either face to face or through the medium of the printed word, video or audio tapes, radio, television, or the Internet.

*Concentration is the secret of strength
in all management of human affairs.*
—Ralph Waldo Emerson

*He had read much, but his contemplation
was much more than his reading. He was
wont to say that if he had read as much
as other men, he should have known
no more than other men.*
—John Aubrey

*One picture is worth more than
ten thousand words.*
—Chinese proverb

Chapter Eight

CONCENTRATION

CHAPTER SUMMARY

Concentration is deliberately keeping our consciousness focused on one thing, one image, or one idea. This is difficult to do because it is contrary to our general evolutionary need to be broadly conscious of as much as possible around us.

Concentration involves two things: filtering out extraneous impressions of the world around us and controlling our mind's natural tendency to flit from one subject to another.

At advanced levels, concentration leads to (1) an awareness that the knowing "I" is distinct from the mind; (2) the ability to distinguish confidently between truth and falsehood; (3) the faculty of intuiting directly rather than knowing only through sensations; and (4) a transcendence of the ordinary lower mind by functioning instead at the higher or causal level.

When we eventually become conscious of the One Self of the universe, we will share its awareness of all things

*in an eternal "now" and "here." Learning to focus on the
here and now helps us toward that goal.*

*Concentration can be helped by choosing an object to con-
centrate on that is attractive to us: a devotional image,
a fascinating concept, a virtue.*

*As we practice concentration, when our mind wanders, as
it inevitably will, we should bring it back gently but
firmly to the object of concentration.*

*A step toward concentration is to practice consecutive think-
ing—following step by step the scenes of a story or the
stages of a process.*

F OR THOSE who are beginning to train their minds,
few things are more taxing than concentration. Concentration is difficult because it is contrary to our in-
grained mental habits.

In the earliest stages of our mental development, our
progress depended on our mind's swift movements, al-
ertness, and readiness to receive impacts from sensation
after sensation, turning its attention quickly from one to
another. At that stage, versatility was necessary, and an
outward-directed attention was essential to survival.

While the mind is collecting materials for thought,
mobility is an advantage. During a great many past lives,
our mind has grown and increased its mobility by such
activity. It naturally comes as a shock when we try to stop
our attention's habitual running outward in every direction and to fix it on a single point. The mind plunges wild-
ly, like an untamed horse when it first feels the bit.

*In this world, if a man sits down to
think, he is immediately asked
if he has the headache.*
—Ralph Waldo Emerson

As already noted, our mental body is shaped into images of the objects that capture our attention. The great authority on Yoga, Patanjali, speaks of stopping the modifications of the thinking principle, that is, of controlling these ever-changing mental reproductions of the outer world. Concentration, on the form side, is stopping the fluctuating modifications of the mental body and keeping it shaped to one steady image. On the life side, the side of the knower, concentration is directing the attention steadily to a form so as to reproduce it perfectly.

When we keep our mind thus shaped to one image by an act of will and we steadily contemplate that image, we achieve a far fuller knowledge of the object than we could from any verbal description of it.

Concentration is not a passive state. On the contrary, it is one of intense and regulated activity. It is a mental effort that resembles tensing the muscles before making a jump. In fact, with beginners, this mental tension always shows itself in a corresponding physical tension; and fatigue of the muscles, not only of the nervous system, follows the exercise of concentration.

By fixing our eyes steadily on an object, we observe details that a hasty glance misses. Similarly, steady concentration enables us to observe the details of an idea. As we increase the intensity of our concentration, we take in more at a time, just as a runner passes more objects in a minute than a walker does.

DIFFICULTIES

As we develop the power of concentration, we have to overcome two difficulties. First, we must learn to cope with the "monkey mind," which is constantly chattering and jumping from one topic to another. We must learn to disregard the random impressions that the mind continually receives; we must resist the tendency to respond to irrelevant outside impressions. To do this we have to direct our attention to the act of resistance itself, but when we have overcome the tendency to respond, this resistance must also pass. Perfect balance is needed, neither resistance nor nonresistance, but a steady quiet so strong that waves from outside produce no result, not even the secondary result of the awareness of something to be resisted.

Second, we must learn to cope with the "cow mind," which chews on ideas like a cow on its cud. For a time, the mind must hold the object of concentration as its sole image and fix itself on that alone. It must not only refuse to modify itself in response to impacts from outside, but also cease its own inner activity of constantly rearranging its contents, mulling over them, establishing new relations, discovering hidden likenesses and differences. Imposing inner stillness is even more difficult than ignoring outside impacts. Our inner world of private thoughts and feelings is more closely identified with ourselves and, in fact, for most people represents their "I." Therefore the mind is especially concerned with its own inner life.

In concentration, mental activity does not cease, but all of it flows in a single channel. Water flowing shallowly over a broad surface has little power. But the same quantity of water passing through a narrow channel with the same initial impulse will carry away an obstacle in its path. Steam allowed to expand in the free air cannot move a fly out of its path, but directed through a pipe, the same steam can drive a piston. Hence the value of the "one-pointedness" that teachers of meditation insist on. A mind that does not jump around to new ideas like a monkey or chew over old ones like a cow transforms its latent power into effective strength.

Even the effort to still the mind brings about a step forward in the evolution of consciousness. It soon brings us to recognize that the ruler and the ruled cannot be one, and thus instinctively to identify ourselves with the ruler. "I quiet my mind" is the expression of the consciousness. So the mind is felt to be a possession of the "I," and not the "I" itself.

DISCOVERING THE KNOWER

The distinction between "I" and "my mind" grows unconsciously until we find ourselves becoming aware of a duality, of something (the "I") that is controlling and something (the mind) that is controlled. We evolve an awareness that the "I" is independent of both body and mind. This is our first direct realization of our true immortal nature, although we may have already conceived the idea intellectually. Such an intellectual conception in fact prompts the concentration that produces the realization.

> *Bringing the mind back again and again to the object of concentration teaches it to concentrate under the stern eye of the will. To command the mind is one thing. To teach it as a willing and happy pupil is quite another.*
>
> —Ernest Wood

As our practice of concentration goes on, we become increasingly aware inwardly, rather than outwardly. Our sense of who we are moves continually inward. Concentration unfolds a power of knowing truth at sight, which shows itself only when the lower mind, with its slow processes of reasoning, is transcended. This power derives from the fact that the "I" is an expression of the One Self, whose nature is knowledge. When the developed knower comes into contact with a truth, the vibrations of that truth are capable of producing a coherent image within the mind, whereas a falsehood causes a distorted image that is disproportionate and by its very reflection announces its distorted nature. It takes, however, a keenly developed awareness before we can rely solely on our inner perception of what is true; meanwhile we must be wary of self-deception.

As the lower mind assumes a more and more subordinate position, the powers of the self assert their own predominance. Intuition, which is analogous to direct vision on the physical plane, supplements an exclusive reliance on reasoning. However, what is often called "intuition" is really instinct or impulse born of desire and is lower, not higher, than reasoning. Again, we must be wary of self-deception, of mistaking some irrational impulse for super-rational insight.

After we have trained the mind to concentrate on an object and maintain its one-pointedness for some little time, the next stage is to drop the object from consciousness. The mind then has an attitude of fixed attention *without being directed to anything*. In this state, the mental body shows no image; its own material is held steady and firm without receiving any impressions, in a condition of perfect calm, like a lake without waves. This state can last for only a very brief period. It is like a chemical "critical state," the point of transition between two substates of matter, such as water and vapor. Consciousness escapes from the mental body, which is stilled, and passes into the causal body of the higher mind.

That passage is through a point of contact between the two bodies called a "laya center." Any two contiguous states of consciousness are connected by such a center, which is a neutral state, neither one nor the other, but a quiet condition between the two. The word *laya* means "dissolution" or "merger" and is used because one state of consciousness has to dissolve before the next can come into activity. An analogy is a pendulum that swings to the right until it reaches its farthest point, then reverses direction and swings back to the left. There is an instant when the pendulum, as it reverses its motion, is moving neither right nor left, but is still. That still instant is like the laya center.

The passage of consciousness between the mental body and the causal body is accompanied by a momentary loss of consciousness—the inevitable result of the disappearance of objects of consciousness—followed by consciousness at the higher level. Thus, the dropping of objects of consciousness in the lower plane is followed by the appearance of objects of consciousness in the higher. After that, the self can shape the lower mental body according to its own thoughts and permeate it with its own vibrations, molding it according to the visions of planes beyond its own, glimpsed at moments of high perception. The mental body is thus able to respond to ideas that otherwise would be inaccessible to it, sometimes in the inspirations of genius that flash down into the mind and illuminate the world. In our ordinary mental state, we can hardly tell how such ideas come, only that they do.

CONSCIOUSNESS BEYOND TIME AND SPACE

A form occupies a particular place. It is closer to or more distant from other forms occupying places different from its own. If a form changes from one place to another, it must cross the intervening space. The passage may be rapid as a lightning flash or sluggish as a turtle, but it must be made. And that movement occupies a period of time, whether brief or long.

For consciousness, however, space and time have no such existence. Consciousness changes its state, not its place. It either knows or does not know about something that is not itself, to the extent that it can or cannot respond to the vibrations of that not-self. Its horizon enlarges with its power to reproduce vibrations. Consciousness does not travel across intermediate space, for space pertains to forms. Forms affect each other most when they are nearest to each other, their power over one another diminishing as the distance between them increases. But that is not the case with consciousness.

*The clarity of my ideas and my ability to prolong my
occupations indefinitely without experiencing fatigue
is explained by my keeping each object and each
business filed in my head as in a chest of drawers.
When I wish to interrupt one occupation, I shut its
drawer and open another. They do not mix, and
when I am busy with one I am not importuned
or tired by the other.... When I want to sleep,
I shut all the drawers, and I am fast asleep.*

—Napoleon

Those who have developed concentration to a high
level discover that space does not exist for consciousness.
Adepts at concentration can acquire knowledge of an
object merely by concentrating on it, and distance is
no barrier. They become conscious of a distant object,
not because their "astral" vision acts telescopically, but
because in one sense the whole universe exists at every
point. These adepts can reach this "Heart of Life" and see
all things in it.

The Chandogya Upanishad (8.1.3) speaks of "the little space within the heart," which is "as great as this vast
universe." This is the immortal Self (or Atma): "Within
this abide the sky and the world; within this abide fire and
air, the sun and the moon, the lightning and the stars, all
that is and all that is not."

"The little space within the heart" is an ancient mys-
tic term for the subtle nature of the Self, which is truly
one and all-pervading, so that anyone who is conscious in

the Self is conscious at all points of the universe. This can be compared to the fact that the movement of a body on Earth affects the farthest stars, because all bodies exist in and are interpenetrated by a continuous field that transmits vibrations to any distance. As this is true of the form side of nature, consciousness, the life side of nature, must similarly be all-pervading and continuous.

We feel ourselves to be "here" at this spot because we are receiving impressions from the objects around us. So when our consciousness vibrates in response to distant objects as fully as it does to near objects, we will feel ourselves to be with them also. If consciousness responds to an event taking place on Mars as fully as to an event taking place in our own room, there is no difference in our knowledge of each, and we feel ourselves to be equally "here" in each case. We as the knower are wherever our consciousness is, and our consciousness includes everything we respond to, everything within our range of vibration.

A physical analogy may be helpful. The eye sees only things that reflect light to it, and nothing else. But it doesn't even see them in their entirety. It can respond only within a certain range of vibrations; everything beyond that range, above or below it, such as ultraviolet or infrared light waves, is invisible to us. If our eye could develop a wider range of vision, it would see things it did not see before, even though they were there all along. Analogies like this illustrate the old Hermetic axiom, "As above, so below." By thinking about something we are familiar with in the world "below," we can often get an idea about something beyond our purview in the world "above." Just as there are physical colors that we cannot see because our eyes are not structured to recognize them, so there are nonphysical realities we cannot perceive with our physical senses.

Being conscious at any place is different from "going to" the higher planes in what is sometimes called "astral travel." In the first case, the self, whether encased in lower vehicles or not, feels at once in the presence of the "distant" objects; in the second case, the self clothed in its mental or astral body travels from point to point and is conscious of the transition. There is a far more important difference, however. In "astral travel," the conscious self may be in the midst of a crowd of objects that it does not in the least understand, a new and strange world that bewilders and confuses it. But when one's consciousness "is" at any place, it understands all that it sees and it knows the life as well as the form. The light of the One Self shines through all, producing a serene knowledge that can never be gained by spending countless ages in the wilderness of forms.

This direct knowing beyond time and space is in the distant evolutionary future for most of us, whose consciousness is conditioned by the space-time continuum in which we exist. But concentration is the means by which the self escapes from the bondage of forms and enters into the freedom of peace. "For him without concentration there is no peace," says the Bhagavad Gita (2.66), for peace has her nest on a rock that towers above the tossing waves of form.

TECHNIQUES OF CONCENTRATION

Having understood the theory of concentration, the student should begin its practice. Those with a devotional temperament will find their work much easier, because they can use the object of their devotion as the object of their contemplation. Since their heart is powerfully attracted to that object, the mind will readily dwell on it, presenting the beloved image without effort and excluding others with equal ease. For the mind is continually impelled by desire, and constantly seeks to present images that give pleasure and to exclude those that give pain. So the mind will dwell on a beloved image, steadied in its contemplation by the pleasure it experiences. If interrupted from contemplation on the image, the mind will return to it again and again.

Devotees can thus easily reach a considerable degree of concentration. They should imagine as clearly as they can a picture or image of their object of devotion. They then keep the mind fixed on that image. A Christian might think of the Christ, of the Virgin Mother, of a patron saint, of a guardian angel; a Hindu might think of the great Lord Shiva, of Vishnu, of Ganesha, of Shri Krishna; a Buddhist might think of the Buddha, of the Bodhisattva; a Parsi, of Ahuramazda, of Mithra. These objects appeal to the devotion of the worshipper, and the attraction they exercise over the heart binds the mind to the object that gives it happiness. In this way, the mind becomes concentrated with the least effort.

Those whose temperament is not devotional can still use the element of attraction as a help, but in their case the mind will be attracted to an idea rather than to a person. The earliest attempts at concentration should always be made with the help of attraction. With the nondevotional, the attractive image may take the form of some profound idea, some high problem, such as the One expressing itself in the manifold glories of the universe or

104

the immensity of space and time. For them the binding power of attraction is their intellectual interest, their deep desire for knowledge, which is one of the profoundest loves of humankind.

Another fruitful object of concentration for those who are not attracted to a personality is a virtue. Virtues may arouse a very effective kind of devotion, for they appeal to the heart through the love of intellectual and moral beauty. The thinker should imagine the virtue in the most complete way possible, first to get a general view of its effects and then to focus on its essential nature. A great subsidiary advantage of this kind of concentration is that, as the mind shapes itself to the virtue and repeats its vibrations, the virtue will gradually become part of the person's nature, and will be firmly established as character.

This shaping of the mind is really an act of self-creation, for after a while the mind falls readily into the forms to which it has been accustomed by concentration, and these forms become its permanent expression. It is true, as written of old (Chandogya Upanishad 3.14.1), that "Man is the creation of thought; what he thinks upon in this life, that, hereafter, he becomes."

When the mind loses concentration on its object, whether devotional or intellectual—as it will do, time after time—it must be brought back and again directed to the object. Often at first the mind will wander without our even noticing it, but suddenly we become aware that our thoughts are dwelling on something other than the chosen object. This will happen again and again, and the mind must patiently be brought back—a wearisome and tiring process. But there is no other way by which concentration can be gained.

A useful and instructive mental exercise, when the mind has thus wandered without our noticing, is to retrace the road along which it traveled as it strayed. This process increases the control of the rider over the runaway horse, and thus diminishes its inclination to escape.

Another technique is consecutive thinking, which is not identical with concentration, though it is related. In consecutive thinking, the mind passes from one to another image of a sequence and is not fixed on one alone. This is far easier than fixed concentration, and the beginner may use it to lead up to the more difficult task. For example, it is often helpful for devotees to select a scene from the life of the one to whom they are devoted, and to picture the scene vividly in all its details, with local surroundings of landscape and color. Thus the mind is gradually steadied on one line of thought, so that it can be led to and finally fixed on the central figure of the scene, the object of devotion.

As the scene is reproduced in the mind, it takes on a feeling of reality, and it is quite possible in this way to get in touch with the akashic record—or the permanent image of that scene on a higher plane—and thus to gain much more knowledge of it than any description can supply. The devotee may also get in touch with the object of devotion and enter into a far more intimate relation with the Beloved than otherwise would be possible. Consciousness is not under the limitations of physical space, but *is* wherever it is conscious.

However, this sequential thinking is not concentration itself. The mind must finally be fastened on the one object of concentration and remain fixed there, not reasoning about it but, as it were, entering into and absorbing its content.

APPLICATIONS

1. The first step in learning to concentrate is to sit quietly. A traditional technique is to concentrate on the breath as it goes in and out of the nostrils. Do not control your breath, but just be aware of it. Do not focus on the movement of your chest, but on the air passing in and out of your nostrils.

2. Experiment with various objects of concentration to find which works best for you. In different sessions of concentration, try different objects: an image or icon, an intellectual concept, a practical virtue, a word or inspiring passage you have memorized for the purpose. What you concentrate on is less important than the act of concentration, so discover what is most effective for you.

3 If you discover that your attention has wandered off on a long chain of associations, it may be helpful to retrace the steps to find your way back to the point of concentration. Or it may be helpful to approach concentration by following a consecutive line of thought with clear stages and steps. But finally the important thing is to work at sustaining a one-pointed focus. For that, it may be best just to break off any wandering thought and bring the mind gently back to the chosen object.

Practice is the best teacher.
—Latin motto

They are never alone that are accompanied with noble thoughts.
—Philip Sidney

Meditation is just the opposite of going to sleep. Sleep, mind-wandering, daydreaming, drift, dullness, and disorder are all absent in meditation.
—Ernest Wood

Chapter Nine

ACHIEVING CONCENTRATION AND MEDITATING

If we have difficulty concentrating, we can help ourselves by constant practice and a calm awareness of those difficulties.

Our mind functions largely by habit, so if we habituate it to concentrating, it will concentrate. It is better not to struggle against intrusive thoughts, but simply to replace them with complementary welcome thoughts.

The physical body tends to echo the mind, so when we concentrate the mind, the body may become tense. This is not desirable and should be counteracted by breaking off the mental concentration and relaxing the body. Concentration should be practiced in short but regular sessions so as not to fatigue either the body or the mind.

Concentration is not an end in itself but is a technique to make meditation possible. Meditating here means contemplating something with the goal of realizing its inner reality rather than its outer form.

Chapter Nine

THE UNIVERSAL COMPLAINT of those who are beginning to practice concentration is that the very attempt to concentrate results in a greater restlessness of the mind. To some extent this is true, for the law of action and reaction works here as everywhere, and the pressure put on the mind causes a corresponding reaction. But we find on closer study that the mind's increase in restlessness is largely illusory. It is due chiefly to the opposition suddenly set up between the self, who wills steadiness, and the mind, in its normal condition of mobility.

For a long series of lives, we as the self have been carried along by the mind and emotions with all their swift movements, just as our bodies are carried through space by the whirling Earth. We are not conscious of the Earth's movement because we are so much a part of it, moving as it moves. If we were able to step off the planet and thus stop our movement on it, we would be conscious that the Earth is moving at a high rate of speed. Similarly, as long as we yield to every movement of the mind, we do not realize its continual activity and restlessness. But when we steady ourselves and stop moving, then we feel the ceaseless motion of the mind in which we have thus far participated.

If beginners in the practice of concentration are aware of this fact, they will not be discouraged in their early efforts, but will recognize the mind's restlessness as a universal experience. Taking it for granted, they will go quietly on with their task. After all, they are only repeating the experience voiced by the epic hero Prince Arjuna thousands of years ago in the Bhagavad Gita (6.33–4):

This Yoga which you have declared to be by equanimity—I see no stable foundation for it, owing to restlessness; for the mind is truly restless. It is impetuous, strong, and difficult to bend; I think it as hard to curb as the wind.

And the answer Krishna gave Arjuna is still true, for it points out the only way to success (6.35):

Without doubt, the mind is hard to curb and restless; but it may be curbed by constant practice and by dispassion.

A mind steadied by constant practice and lack of passion will not be so easily thrown off balance by the restless crowd of wandering thoughts from other minds that continually bombard us, constantly seeking to enter our consciousness. For the mind used to concentration always retains a certain positiveness and is not readily shaped by uninvited intruders.

UNWANTED THOUGHTS

People with weak self-control are indiscriminatively receptive to whatever thoughts impinge on their minds. All of us need to learn how we can make ourselves normally "positive" or receptive to thoughts, and also how we can become "negative" or nonreceptive when we decide it is useful to be so.

The habit of concentration by itself tends to strengthen the mind and helps it to exercise control and selection among the thoughts that come to it from outside. But in addition, those who are training their minds should maintain an attitude of steady watchfulness over uninvited thoughts and should constantly exercise selection.

Living, as we all do, in a continual current of both helpful and harmful thoughts, we need to cultivate an automatic selection by the mind. Refusing to harbor unwanted thoughts, promptly transforming them by replacing them by ones of the opposite character—after a time such practices tune the mind to automatically draw in helpful thoughts and neutralize harmful ones. The mind is like a magnet, attracting and repelling thoughts, but we can determine what it attracts and repels.

The "repelling" of harmful thoughts is not simply ignoring them or rejecting them or pretending they were never there. If we are to have power over our thoughts, we must be aware of what thoughts we have. When we recognize that a thought is harmful, we should acknowledge its existence, and then neutralize its energy by deliberately replacing it with a helpful thought. This is not the repression of harmful thoughts, but their transmutation into something else.

If we watch the thoughts that come into our minds, we find that we encourage those that are congruous with our habitual mental activities. If, for a time, we deliberately practice selection, the mind soon selects by itself along the lines we have laid down for it; objectionable thoughts do not penetrate. Harmonious, rhythmical vibrations reject the inharmonious and irregular, which fly off from the rhythmically vibrating surface of the mental body as a pebble does when it strikes a whirling wheel.

Habit is a sort of second nature.
—Cicero

Habit is overcome by habit.
—Thomas à Kempis

However, in fighting against anything, the very force we send out causes a corresponding reaction and thus increases our trouble. Therefore, when an unwanted thought enters the mind, it may be better not to fight it directly, but to utilize the fact that the mind can think of only one thing at a time. If we turn the mind immediately to a helpful thought, the harmful one is expelled, as turning the eye to an object in a different direction causes the image of the first object to drop from the field of vision. Some people waste years combating thoughts that bother them, whereas quietly occupying the mind with helpful thoughts leaves no room for its assailants. As the mind draws to itself matter that does not respond to disagreeable thoughts, it gradually becomes receptive to desirable ones and unreceptive to unwanted kinds.

This is the secret of right receptivity. The mind responds according to its habitual state; it resonates with everything that is harmonious with it. Disagreeable thoughts stick to a disagreeable nature; they slide off a polished mind. By habitual good thinking, we make the mind positive to helpful thoughts and negative to harmful ones, thus building into its very fabric materials that are receptive only to helpfulness. We must think of what we desire to receive and refuse to think of what we desire not to receive. Such a mind draws to itself helpful thoughts from the thought atmosphere surrounding it and repels the others, thus growing ever stronger in helpfulness. Another mind that has been habituated to harmful thoughts attracts such thoughts and consequently grows ever more negative.

We can use the method of replacing one thought by another to great advantage in many ways. If an unkind thought about someone enters the mind, replace it at once by a thought of some good quality the person has or of some good action they have done. If the mind is oppressed by anxiety, turn it to the thought of the purpose that runs through life, the Good Law that "mightily and sweetly ordereth all things." If a particular kind of undesirable thought persistently obtrudes, then it is wise to use a special defense—some verse or phrase that embodies the opposite idea. Whenever the objectionable thought presents itself, this phrase should be repeated and dwelled upon. In a week or two the thought will cease to trouble.

It is a good plan constantly to furnish the mind with some high thought, some word of cheer, some inspiration to noble living. Before going out into life's turmoil each day, we should give the mind this shield of good thought. A few strengthening words from some inspired piece of writing are enough. If they are fixed in the mind by a few repetitions in the early morning, they will recur again and again during the day and will repeat themselves whenever the mind is otherwise unengaged.

RIGHT AND WRONG CONCENTRATION

The beginner should be wary of certain dangers connected with the practice of concentration, because many eager students, in their wish to go far, go too fast, and so hinder instead of helping themselves. The body is apt to suffer through ignorance and inattention.

When people begin to concentrate mentally, the body puts itself into a state of tension, which is involuntary and not noticed. But we can become aware of the body's reflection of the mind's activity in trivial things: an effort to remember causes the forehead to wrinkle, the eyes to become fixed, and the eyebrows to be drawn down. Tense attention is accompanied by a fixed stare; and anxiety by an eager, wistful gaze. Efforts of the mind are followed by efforts of the body. The muscles become rigid and the nerves are set on edge. As a result, physical fatigue is apt to follow, with muscular and nervous exhaustion and headache. Thus people are led to give up the practice of concentration, believing that these ill effects are inevitable.

As a matter of fact, the undesirable effects can be avoided by a simple precaution. Beginners should break off concentration from time to time to pay attention to the state of their body. If they find it strained, tense, or rigid, they should at once relax. Doing this several times breaks the association between mental and bodily concentration, and the body then remains pliant and resting while the mind is concentrated. The body cannot help the mind by its tension. It can only injure itself. As Patanjali said, in meditation the posture adopted should be "easy and pleasant."

A personal anecdote may illustrate this point. One day, while Annie Besant was under H. P. Blavatsky's training, HPB asked her to make an effort of the will. She did so with great intensity, with the result that the blood vessels of her head started to swell. "My dear," HPB said dryly, "you do not will with your blood vessels."

115

Concentration should be practiced sparingly at first and should never be carried to the point of brain fatigue. A few minutes at a time is enough for a beginning, with the time lengthened gradually as the practice goes on. But, however short the time, practice should be regular. If a day is missed, the previous condition of the mind reasserts itself, and the work has to be recommenced. Practice that is steady and regular, but not prolonged, ensures the best results and avoids danger.

In some schools of Hatha Yoga, students are instructed to assist their concentration by fixing their eyes on a black spot on a white wall, and to maintain this fixity of gaze until trance results. This should not be done for two reasons. First, after a while the practice causes the eyes temporarily to lose their power of adjustment. Second, it brings about a form of temporary brain paralysis, beginning with fatigue of the retinal cells of the eye. As the waves of light beat on these cells and the spot disappears from view, the place on the retina where the image is formed becomes insensitive as a result of prolonged response. This fatigue spreads inward until finally a kind of paralysis can result, and the person passes into a hypnotic trance. In fact, excessive stimulation of a sense organ such as the eyes—by means of a revolving mirror, a swinging pendulum, or the like—is a recognized means in the West for producing hypnosis.

The highest possible stage in moral culture is when we recognize that we ought to control our thoughts.
—Charles Darwin

Brain paralysis not only stops all thinking on the physical plane but renders the brain insensitive to non-physical vibrations, so that the self cannot impress it. Such trance states do not set us free, but merely deprive us of our instrument. A person may remain for weeks in a trance thus induced, but awake no wiser than at the beginning of the trance. Such trance does not produce knowledge; it merely wastes time. Such methods do not increase spiritual power; they merely bring about physical disability.

MEDITATION

Meditation in the tradition of Patanjali is the sustained attitude of a mind concentrated on an object of devotion, a problem that needs illumination, or anything we want to realize in its inner life rather than its outer form.

We cannot effectively meditate until we have adequately mastered concentration. Concentration is not an end in itself, but a means to an end; it fashions the mind into an instrument that can be used at the will of its owner. When a concentrated mind is steadily directed to any object, with a view to piercing the veil that separates the outer from the inner reality, reaching the life within, and drawing that life into union with the life behind the mind, then meditation is performed. Concentration makes the mind one-pointed; meditation directs the mind to dwell steadily on any object of which inner knowledge is desired.

Anyone who decides to lead a spiritual life must devote some time each day to meditation. As we cannot sustain physical life without food, so we cannot sustain spiritual life without meditation. We need to devote half an hour or so a day to shutting out the world and receiving a current of life from the spiritual planes. Only to the mind that is concentrated, steady, and shut out from the world, can the Divine reveal itself. The One Divine Self appears in the universe in endless forms; but within the human heart, it shows itself as the heart's very life and nature; the Divine is revealed to that which is a fragment of itself.

In the silence, peace and strength flow into the soul, so that whoever is efficient in meditation is efficient in the world as well. Practical mysticism is the greatest force in the world. Concentrated intelligence combined with the power of withdrawing from turmoil means immensely increased energy in work and in steadiness, self-control, and serenity. Those proficient in meditation waste no time, scatter no energy, miss no opportunity. They govern events because within themselves is the power of which events are only the outer expression. Through meditation we share the Divine life, and therefore share the Divine power.

APPLICATIONS

1. When you are trying to concentrate, or whenever some unwelcome thought comes into your mind, do not fight against it, but turn your attention immediately to an opposite, welcome thought. Practice doing this in your sessions of concentration and meditation.

2. Memorize a number of short affirmations, invocations, or aphorisms, and begin each day by saying one. If at any time during the day your mind is unoccupied, repeat the saying silently to yourself. An example is the following:

   From the unreal, lead me to the real,
   From darkness, lead me to light,
   From death, lead me to immortality.
   Peace to all beings.

3. As in the practice of concentration, sit comfortably with your back straight and your feet flat on the floor. Close your eyes. Relax and take a few deep breaths. Then visualize an image such as the Christ or the Buddha, a beautiful scene, or a rose. Or repeat silently one of the passages you have memorized. Spend a few minutes contemplating the image or the passage. Then deliberately send out thoughts of peace and goodwill to the world or to someone you know to be in need of help. Then be still inwardly for a brief period. Open your eyes and slowly bring your consciousness back to your present surroundings.

Study to be quiet.
—Saint Paul

*A hundred load of worry will
not pay an ounce of debt.*
—George Herbert

It is not work that kills, but worry.
—English proverb

*Thinking. Chattering to myself.
Avoiding silence.*
—Sam Keen

Chapter Ten

STRENGTHENING THE POWER OF THOUGHT

CHAPTER SUMMARY

Developing thought power has two complementary aspects: we train our mental body and we activate abilities that are fully available but in a latent state. To be active, those innate abilities of quick understanding and logical, orderly thinking have to function through a trained mental body.

Worry is the purposeless repetition of thoughts about a problem. We can overcome such repetition by deliberately replacing the worrying thoughts with thoughts of confidence, calmness, and trust in the orderliness of the cosmos.

Strengthening our thought power involves not just learning to think clearly, but also not to think at all. Our minds need a rest from time to time. That rest can come from either a cessation of thought or a change of thought to a quite different subject.

*How very commonly we hear it remarked
that such and such thoughts are beyond the
compass of words! I do not believe that
any thought, properly so called, is out
of the reach of language.*
—Edgar Allan Poe

A NY STUDY that does not lead to practice is barren. And that is especially true for the study of thought power, which has a very practical application. The old adage mentioned earlier still holds good. The purpose of philosophy is to put an end to pain. We can learn first to develop and then to use our thought power for various aspects of that purpose.

One use of thought power is helping ourselves and also those around us—both the living and the dead. We are all connected in the vast web of existence, so everything we do and every thought we have affects others. One of the great teachers wrote, "Your karma, good or bad, being one and the common property of all mankind, nothing good or bad can happen to you that is not shared by many others." Another purpose for which we can use thought power is to quicken human evolution, including our own progress.

It is a law of life that growth results from exercise. We develop new ways of more fully expressing our life by exercising the faculties we have. Thought power can be increased only by steadily and persistently exercising it.

Just as muscular development depends on the exercise of the muscles we already possess, so mental development depends on the exercise of the mind that is already ours.

Life is constantly seeking to express itself outwardly in increasing ways through the forms in which it is embodied. The pressure by the life force on its forms causes the forms to expand, and fresh matter is laid down. In this way, part of the expansion is made permanent. When a muscle is exercised, more life flows into it, the cells multiply, and the muscle grows. When the mental body vibrates under the action of thought, fresh matter is drawn in from the mental atmosphere around it and is built into the mental body, which thus increases in size as well as in complexity of structure. So a mental body that is continually exercised grows. The direction of its growth depends on the quality of its thought, whether subtle or crass, good or bad, and the extent of its growth depends on the amount of thought it produces.

Both the mental body and the physical brain improve by exercise, and if we want them to do so, we have to engage in regular daily thinking of a kind that will improve their capacities. In addition, our latent powers of quick understanding and logical, orderly thinking also evolve more rapidly by such exercise and can thus interact more fully with the vehicles of the brain and mental body.

To have its full effect, any practice must be methodical. Choose a good book containing fresh ideas on some subject that appeals to you. Read a sentence or two slowly, and then think carefully and intently about what you have read. It is a good rule to think twice as long as you read, because the purpose of this reading is not simply to acquire knowledge but to strengthen the thinking faculties. Give half an hour a day to this practice if you can, but you might start with a quarter of an hour, if you find that your attention tires at first. If you follow this practice regularly for a few months, at the end of that time you will be conscious of a distinct growth in mental strength. You will find yourself able to deal with the ordinary problems of life more effectively than before. If we want the reward of increased mental ability, we have to earn it by hard thinking.

The work of earning that reward is, as already pointed out, twofold. On the one hand, we activate the latent powers of our consciousness; on the other hand, we develop the forms through which our consciousness expresses itself. We need to keep the first in mind. Many people recognize that clear thinking improves the connections in the brain, but they are not aware that the source of all thought is the unborn, undying Self, and that we are only making active what we already have latently.

Our Inner Powers

Within us are all the powers of the Self, for the divine Self is the root of the life of each of us. So we only need to learn how to use those powers. The aspect of the Self that is the ability to know lives in everyone and is constantly seeking opportunities for fuller expression. Its power is within us, uncreated, eternal; the forms we use are molded and changed by our use of them, but our life is the Self, illimitable in its powers. That power within each of us is the same power that shapes the universe; it is Divine, not human, an inseparable portion of the life of the Logos, the divine intelligence that governs the world.

If we realize that our inner powers are available and remember that the problem lies in our lack of skill in applying them, we will work with more courage and hope and therefore with more efficiency. Our essential nature is knowledge, but how far this nature will find expression during our present incarnation depends on us. Its expression is indeed limited by how we have thought in the past (our conditioning), but by our thinking in the present we can increase and make more efficient the expression of the inner knowing that is part of our essence. Forms are plastic and can be remolded, although slowly, by the vibrations of the life within them.

Above all, regularity of practice is essential for steady growth. When we skip a day's practice, we need three or four days' work to compensate for our backsliding, at least during the earlier stages of growth. After we have acquired a habit of steady thought, our regularity of practice is less important. But until that habit is established, regularity is essential, for if the old habit of loose drifting reasserts itself, the matter of the mental body falls back into its old loosely organized shapes. Then we have to shake it out of this condition all over again when we resume our practice. Better five minutes of work done regularly than half an hour on some days and none on others.

There are two days in the week about which I never worry. One is Yesterday. The other is Tomorrow.
—Robert Jones Burdette

Chapter Ten

WORRY, ITS MECHANISM
AND ERADICATION

People age more by worry than by work. Mental work, unless excessive, does not injure the mind but strengthens it. However, the mental process known as "worry" certainly injures it and after a time can exhaust us and make us so irritable that steady mental work becomes impossible.

Worry is the process of repeating the same train of thought over and over again with small alterations, coming to no conclusion and without even the aim of reaching a conclusion. The mental body and the brain, not the consciousness, initiate this continued reproduction of thought forms, but they impose the repeated thoughts on the consciousness. As overtired muscles cannot keep still but twitch restlessly even against the will, so the tired mental body and brain repeat over and over again the very vibrations that have wearied them, although the thinker vainly tries to quiet them in order to rest. This is inertia, the tendency to continue moving in a direction already begun.

For example, we have been thinking about how to solve a difficult problem and tried to find a useful solution. We have failed to do so and have stopped trying, but we remain dissatisfied, wanting a solution and preoccupied by fear of anticipated trouble. This fear keeps us in an anxious and restless condition, causing an irregular outflow of energy. Then under the impulse of this energy, the mental body and brain, undirected by us as thinker, continue to throw up the images already shaped and rejected. These images are forced on our attention, and the cycle recurs again and again. As weariness increases, irritability sets in and reacts again on the already wearied mental body and brain, and so action and reaction continue in a vicious circle. In worry, the thinker is slave to the servant bodies and suffers under their tyranny.

Every type of thought makes a form for itself or digs a channel in our mental landscape, so new thoughts tend to follow the same patterns as old ones, because that is the line of least resistance. Thus a thought that causes pain recurs just as readily as a thought that gives pleasure. The object of fear or pleasure, the picture of what will happen if anticipation becomes reality, makes a mind channel or a mold for thought in the mental body and also a track in the brain. When they are free from other activity, the mental body and the brain tend to repeat old forms and to let unused energy flow into the channels already made.

We can escape from the vicious circle of worry begetting worry. The very automatism of the mental body and brain, their tendency to repeat vibrations already produced, can be used to correct the useless repetition of thoughts that cause pain.

A good way to get rid of a "worry channel" is to dig another of exactly opposite character. We make such a channel by clear, persistent, regular thought. We should give three or four minutes in the morning, when we first wake up, to some encouraging thought, such as "The Self is peace; that Self am I. The Self is strength; that Self am I." We can think that in our innermost nature we are one with the Supreme; and in that nature we are undying, unchanging, fearless, serene, and strong. We can think that, although clothed in perishable bodies that feel the sting of pain and the gnawing of anxiety, we are not those bodies, but a free spirit that has donned them. As we immerse ourselves in such thoughts, peace will enfold us, and we will feel it as our own, as our natural atmosphere.

The thought of the Self that is peace and strength will become habitual, and worry will be a thing of the past.

Another way to overcome worry is to train the mind to rest in the Good Law of universal order or karma, which justly balances and harmonizes all the energies we have sent out in the past. Confidence in that Law establishes a habit of contentment. In this case we dwell on the thought that all circumstances work within the Law that governs the universe and that nothing happens by chance. Only what the Law brings can reach us, by whatever hand it may come outwardly. Nothing can injure us that is not our due, brought to us by our own thinking, willing, and acting in the past. Whatever we are or experience in our present life is the result of our own choices and decisions in the past. Whatever we choose and decide in the present will determine the circumstances of our future, in this life and others to come.

Even if anticipation of pain or trouble comes to the mind, we will do well to face it calmly, accept it, agree to it. Most of the sting disappears when we acquiesce to the Law, whatever its effects may be. It may also help if we remember that karma always works to free us from the debts that keep us in prison. Though it may bring us pain, that pain can be the way to happiness. Pain, rightly responded to, can break the bonds that keep us tied to the whirling wheel of births and deaths.

What is the hardest task in the world?
To think.
—Ralph Waldo Emerson

When such thoughts have become habitual, the mind ceases to worry, for the claws of worry can find no hold on the strong armor of peace.

THINKING AND STOPPING THOUGHT

We can gain strength by learning both to think and to cease thinking at will. While we are thinking, we should throw our whole mind into the thought and think our best. But when the work of thought is over, it should be dropped completely and not allowed to drift on vaguely, leaving the mind like an unsteered boat knocking against a rock. No one keeps a machine running when it is not being used, needlessly wearing it out. But the priceless machinery of the mind is allowed to turn and turn aimlessly, wearing itself out without purpose.

Learning to let the mind rest is an ability of the greatest value. As our tired limbs luxuriate when stretched in rest, so the tired mind can find comfort in complete rest. Constant thinking means constant vibration; constant vibration means constant waste of energy. Exhaustion results from this useless expenditure. We can use both our mental body and our brain better if we learn to cease thinking when thought is not being directed to useful ends.

Stopping thought is by no means easy. Perhaps it is even more difficult than thinking clearly. The normal state of the mind is to run on, and if we are not directing it, it automatically runs in random directions. But the great authority on mind-control, Patanjali, tells us that a different state is possible—not easy, but possible and helpful. We may never be able to stop the thought process completely, but conscious efforts toward that aim can have beneficial results.

We should practice stopping our thought for very brief periods until we have established the habit, for at first an expenditure of force is needed to hold the mind still. After thinking steadily for a while, drop the thought, and turn the attention away from anything that appears in the mind, persistently rejecting each intruder. If need be, imagine a void as a step to quiescence, and try to be conscious only of stillness and darkness. Persistent practice along these lines will reveal the benefit of the practice, and the resulting sense of quiet and peace will encourage you to persist.

Stopping thought, which is usually busily engaged in outward activities, is a necessary preliminary to work on the higher planes. When the brain has learned to be quiet, when it no longer restlessly throws up the broken images of past activities, then the possibility opens for us to withdraw our consciousness from its physical vesture so that it can be freely active on those higher planes. Those who hope to take this step within their present life must learn to cease thinking, for only when "the modifications of the thinking principle" are checked on the lower plane can freedom on the higher be achieved.

CHANGING THE
SUBJECT OF THOUGHT

Another way of giving rest to the mental body and the brain—much easier than stopping thought—is to change what we are thinking about. If we have spent a long time in some close visual work like reading, our eyes become weary from focusing at close range. We can rest our eyes by closing them (which is like stopping thought) or by refocusing them on some distant scene out a window or even across the room. The refocusing of our eyes at a different range is like changing the object of our thought.

Those who think strenuously and persistently along one line should have a second line of thought, as different as possible from the first, to turn to for refreshment. The extraordinary freshness and youthfulness of thought for which the Victorian British Prime Minister William Gladstone was famous in his old age largely resulted from his secondary intellectual activities. His strongest and most persistent thought went to politics, but his studies in theology and in Greek filled many a leisure hour. Though the world cannot be said to be much richer for his theological pronouncements, his own brain was kept fresh and receptive by these and by his Greek studies.

Charles Darwin, on the other hand, lamented in his old age that he had allowed all of his interests outside his own specialized work to atrophy. Literature and art for him had no attraction, and he keenly felt the limitations he had imposed on himself by overabsorption in one line of study. We all need a change in the exercise of thought as well as of body, or else we may suffer from mental cramp as some people do from writer's cramp.

It is especially important for those absorbed in worldly pursuits to engage their mind in subjects other than business or political activities—subjects related to art, science, or literature, in which they can find mental recreation and improvement. Above all, young people should adopt some such pursuit, before their fresh and active brains grow jaded and weary. If they do, then in old age they will find resources within themselves to enrich and brighten their days. The brain and mental body will preserve their elasticity for a much longer period of time if they have been given periodic rest by a change of focus.

APPLICATIONS

1. Establish a particular time of day, a particular length of time (it can be quite brief, five to fifteen minutes, no more), and a particular place to meditate, to study, or to do some particular mental task. Keep that schedule faithfully for a month. Be as consistent and regular as you can.

2. If you find yourself beginning to worry about something (that is, aimlessly going over a problem), take a deep breath, and repeat to yourself the words of St. Julian of Norwich: "All shall be well, and all shall be well, and all shall be well," or those of Dante: "His will is our peace," or of the gospel of St. Matthew: "Which of you by taking thought can add one cubit unto his stature. Consider the lilies of the field, how they grow; they toil not, neither do they spin. Yet even Solomon in all his glory was not arrayed like one of these."

3. Practice not thinking for a brief period. One way to do that is a technique called "just sitting." Sit still and be alert; keep your mind free of any particular thought; be aware only of sitting.

When your mind starts to slip off on some line of thought, clear it and return to simple awareness. Just sit.

4. Everyone needs a hobby or an avocation for relief from normal routine, something different for relaxation and variety. If you don't already have one, take up such a hobby: hiking, bird watching, golf, stamp collecting, crossword puzzles, gardening, or whatever appeals.

One thought fills immensity.
—William Blake

Three helping one another bear the burden of six.
—George Herbert

*Forget yourself, only to remember
the good of other people.*
—Kuthumi Lal Singh

Chapter Eleven

HELPING OTHERS
BY THOUGHT

CHAPTER SUMMARY

*We can help others by imaging them clearly and sending
them clear, strong, encouraging thoughts, particularly
for whatever they need; but those thoughts should be of
a general nature, never an effort to control or impose
our ideas.*

*We can also help the dead, especially the newly dead,
by sending them loving and supportive thoughts, a practice in accordance with many traditional religious
customs.*

*We can solve our own problems and help others as well while
we are asleep, if we formulate clearly and objectively
the problem to be solved or the situation to be helped as
we are going to sleep.*

*Thought power exercised by people working together coher-
ently in a group is greater than merely a combination of
the thoughts of separate individuals. Group thought is
stronger than individual thought.*

Chapter Eleven

WE OURSELVES benefit greatly from a wise exercise of the power of thought by increasing our mental ability, focusing our will in appropriate directions, and improving our ability to act creatively. But the most valuable ability we gain from developing thought power is our ability to help others. Although the process of developing our power of thought enables us to think clearly about ourselves and our concerns, the best reason for such development is thought for the good of others.

Even an isolated kind thought is helpful to some degree, but we can do far more than merely drop a crumb to the starving. Suppose we want to help a friend who is under the sway of an addiction or any powerful habit. We should sit down alone and first "center" ourselves, that is, identify our consciousness, not with our personality or even with our individual self, but instead with the One Self, the source of all life, which is present in our deepest being. For it is not we who are the agents in this process, but the One Life itself; we do not "fix" things, but are only channels through which the healing and restoring energies of Life can flow.

Having eliminated as far as possible the personal element from our thought and any notion that we know what is right for our friend, we should picture the friend as vividly as we can, as though we were sitting in front of that person. It is helpful if the picture is clear and detailed, so that we see the image as we would see the actual person. This clear picturing, though not essential, makes the process more effective.

We should next fix our attention on this image and address it, with all the concentration we are capable of. We should present good and helpful thoughts, one by one and slowly. Particularly we should hold in our mind a vivid picture of our friend in a state of wholeness, freedom, and health. These thoughts, if formed clearly and energized strongly, will reach our friend as comforting and strengthening influences. Our friend will identify unconsciously with that image and respond to the helpful qualities and ideas by reproducing them.

The success of this practice depends on several factors. One is the degree of our concentration and the steadiness of our thought; the effect will be proportionate, in part, to the development of our thought power. Another is the receptivity of our friend. Receptivity is greatest during sleep, but in the realm of thought, time is no more a limitation than space is; so the effort can have its effect whenever conditions are right. Other factors also play a part, such as our friend's own will and karma.

We must take great care never to suppose that we know what is best for another person or to try to control the other's will in any way. That is why we begin by centering ourselves in the One Life, so that it is not we who work, but Life that works through us. If we try to impose on another a particular kind of behavior, even if our attempt succeeds and even if we are right in what we think is good for the other, little will be gained. The other person's mental tendency toward harmful action will not be changed. Checked in one direction, it will turn to another, and a new weakness will supplant the old. Those who are forcibly constrained from wrong action through another person's domination of their will are no more cured than if they were locked up in prison.

Chapter Eleven

*After the verb "To Love," "To Help" is
the most beautiful verb in the world.*
—Bertha von Suttner

THE ROLE OF KARMA

Apart from the ineffectiveness of trying to force
others to behave in a certain way, we should never try
to impose our will on another, even in order to make that
person do what we think is right. Growth is not helped
by external coercion; real gains come from a convinced
intelligence and purified emotions. But even more important, we do not know what is really best for another,
and to suppose that we do may produce more harm than
good. We can do our best for them, but the result is
always in their hands and in the infallible working of
karma, the Good Law.

We will do no harm if we try according to our best
lights, but we should recognize that our lights may be
dim. We should also have no attachment to the results
of our efforts, whether the result is what we think of as
success or failure. We may, if the circumstances are favorable, be of help, whatever result we see.

Many kinds of help can be given in this same way.
A strong wish for someone's good, sent as a general pro-
tection, will remain around the person as a thought form
for a time proportionate to the strength of the thought. It
will guard the person against negative forces, acting as a
barrier to hostile thoughts and even warding off physical
dangers.

A thought of peace and consolation similarly can soothe and calm the mind, spreading around the person to whom it is sent an atmosphere of calm. A thought of healing and of bodily and spiritual wholeness can also assist the other's recovery from illness.

Prayer often provides help of this same kind. Prayer is frequently more effective than ordinary good wishes because of the greater concentration and intensity that a believer adds to the prayer. Similar concentration and intensity would bring about similar results without the use of a petition, which is typical of much spontaneous prayer. However, prayer is sometimes effective in another way. It may call the attention of some superhuman or evolved human intelligence to the person for whom it is offered. Religious traditions tell of angels and saints, or even of God in some form or other, responding to prayers. Those traditions, although expressed in the images of a particular culture, refer to a real response to prayer: direct aid given by a power surpassing that of the one who prays.

As long as we don't try to impose our wills—even our goodwill—we should never refrain from giving thought assistance through meditation or prayer, or any other sort of assistance for that matter, out of fear that we may be "interfering with karma." Leave karma to take care of itself, and have no more fear of interfering with it than of interfering with gravity.

If we can help a friend, we should do so fearlessly, confident that, if help is within our friend's karma, we may be the happy agents of the Law. If karma does not permit the help, we have done no harm to our friend, and we have still done good in the world by adding helpful thoughts to the general mental atmosphere, from which others may benefit.

For a man to help another is to be a god.
—Pliny the Elder

HELPING THE DEAD

All that we can do for the living by thought we can do even more effectively for those who have gone through death's gateway, for in their case there is no heavy physical matter to be set vibrating before the thought can reach the consciousness. According to the traditions of many religions, the after-death state has several stages. Theosophy identifies the two principal ones as a relatively short stay in the emotional or "astral" world, which is a process of purification or preparation, and a relatively long stay in the mental world, which is a sort of "heaven" experience, before rebirth in a new physical body. It is during the first stage that the living can help the dead.

According to some Eastern teachers, immediately after death has been passed through, the newly dead person tends to focus attention inward, living in the mind rather than in an external world. The thought currents that used to rush outward, seeking the external world through the sense organs, are now blocked by an emptiness caused by the disappearance of the physical body. It is as though someone rushing toward an accustomed bridge over a ravine was suddenly stopped by a bridgeless gulf, the bridge having vanished.

After the loss of the physical body, the matter of the emotional (or "astral") body, in which the dead person then functions, is rearranged. It forms an enclosing shell instead of the pliable instrument it was during physical life. This shell tends to shut in the mental energies and to prevent their outer expression, so the consciousness within it is in a kind of dream state.

The higher and purer the earth life just ended, the more complete is the barrier against intrusive impressions from outside or the emergence of energy from within. But the person whose outward-going emotional energies are thus checked is all the more receptive to influences from the mental world, and can therefore be helped, cheered, and counseled far more effectively by thought than when that person was on earth.

In the world into which those freed from the physical body have gone, a loving thought is as palpable as a loving word or tender caress is here. Everyone who passes over should, therefore, be followed by thoughts of love and peace, by aspirations for swift passage onward through the valley of death to the bright land beyond. All human beings are connected with one another at a deep level and so during life can help one another in many ways. So too the living and the dead remain connected, and help can cross the border of death.

If people on earth knew how much comfort and happiness the wayfarers to the heavenly worlds received from thoughts of love and cheer—if they knew the force their thoughts, like angelic messengers, have to strengthen and console—none would be left lonely by those who remain behind. The beloved dead surely have a claim on our love and care. Even apart from this, how great is the consolation to our hearts, bereft of the presence that gave sunshine to life, to be able still to serve loved ones, and surround them on their way by the guardian angels of thought.

As angels in some brighter dreams
Call to the soul when man doth sleep,
So some strange thoughts transcend
   our wonted themes
And into glory peep.
                —Henry Vaughan

The founders of the great religions were mindful of this service due from those left on earth to those who have passed onward. Hindus have their shraddha or ceremony, by which they help on their way the souls who have passed into the next world, quickening their passage into Svarga, or the heavenly abode. Christian churches have masses and prayers for the dead: "Grant them, O Lord, eternal peace, and let light perpetual shine upon them." Confucians make offerings to the souls of their ancestors and have shrines to commemorate them. Recognizing our connections with the dead is part of recognizing our connection with all life.

THOUGHT WORK OUT OF THE BODY

We don't have to confine our thought activities to the hours we spend in the physical world, for we can do a great deal of effective work by thought while our bodies are lying peacefully asleep. The process of going to sleep is simply the withdrawal of our consciousness from the physical body, as the self passes into the astral world. There, freed from our physical body, we are much more powerful in the effects we can produce by thought. But for the most part in the astral sleep world, we do not send our thought outward, but keep it within ourselves on subjects that interest us in our waking life. Our thought energies run in accustomed grooves and continue to work on the problems that our waking consciousness is trying to solve.

The proverb that "the night brings counsel," like the advice "to sleep on it" when an important decision needs to be made, are vague intuitions of our mental activity during the hours of slumber. In that state, without any deliberate attempt to use the intelligence freed from the distractions of brain consciousness, we can gather and harvest the fruits of its labor.

Those, however, who seek to steer their evolution, instead of allowing it to drift, can consciously benefit from the greater powers they can exercise when they are unimpeded by the weight of the body. The way to do this is simple. When we are going to sleep, we can hold quietly in mind any problem that needs a solution. It must not be debated or argued, but simply stated and left, because debate and argument will prevent sleep. A simple statement is enough to give the required direction to our thought, so that the thinker will take it up and deal with it when freed from the physical body.

The solution will generally be in our mind when we wake up, for the thinker will have impressed it on the brain. It is a good idea to keep paper and pencil by the bed to write down the solution immediately on waking. Ideas that come to us in this way are easily erased by the thronging stimuli from the physical world, and then they are not easy to recover. Many a difficulty in life can be seen clearly in this way and solved when submitted to the intelligence not weighed down by the dense brain.

In much the same way during our sleep, we can help friends in this world or in the next. We can picture our friends and determine to find and help them. The mental image we form will draw us together to communicate with each other in the astral world. But if any emotion is aroused by the thought of the friend—as in the case of one who has passed on—we must become calm before going to sleep. For emotion causes a swirl in the astral body, and if that body is agitated, it isolates the consciousness and makes it impossible for mental vibrations to pass outward.

In some cases of such communication in the astral world, we may remember a dream when we wake up, whereas in others no trace may appear. A dream can be the record—often confused and mixed with other vibrations—of a meeting out of the body. But it does not matter if no trace appears in the brain, because the activities of the freed intelligence are not hindered by the failure of the brain to be aware of them. Our usefulness in the astral world is not governed by how well we remember our dreams. Those memories may be entirely absent, even though very beneficial work occupied the hours of our body's sleep.

THE POWER OF COMBINED THOUGHT

Another form of thought work can be done by a group of people united to help good causes and public movements that benefit humanity. When a group of people think together in a focused way, they can invoke currents of aid from the higher planes. The strength of those currents depends on the size of the group, its coherence, its enthusiasm, and its awareness of the process in which it is engaged. The increased force that comes from the united thought of a group is recognized not only by students of thought power, but by all who know anything about the deeper science of the mind.

It has been the custom, at least among some Christians, to use sustained thinking to help a mission about to evangelize some district. A small group of Roman Catholics, for instance, may meet together for some weeks or months before a mission is sent out in order to prepare the spiritual ground where the mission is going to work. They may imagine the place, thinking of themselves as present there, and then intently meditate on doctrines or symbols of the Church. In this way a thought atmosphere is created in that district that is favorable to the spread of the doctrines, and receptive persons in the district are prepared to wish for instruction.

All religions that practice congregational worship implicitly recognize that a gathering together of two or three, or a much larger number, has a powerful effect on the worshippers, but also on the general mental and spiritual atmosphere. Secular gatherings for sports events, political rallies, entertainment, or any shared interest also have an effect on the mental atmosphere that does not merely sum up the thought power of the individual participants, but multiplies it.

As threads that are individually weak can be braided into a strong rope, so individuals with limited thought power can join in a group effort that is strengthened by their interaction. When earnest people generate thought collectively, whether or not they are in each other's physical presence, they can achieve results that are far beyond the physical effort they expend.

Applications

1. Follow the suggestions in the early part of this chapter to send healing and helping thoughts to someone you know to be in need. Be careful to begin by centering yourself. Do not to try to impose any particular outcome or affect a situation in any particular way. The person you have in mind may be either someone living or someone who has died.

2. When you have a problem to solve or a decision to make, follow the suggestions in the third section of this chapter. Just before you go to sleep, clearly and unemotionally formulate a problem you need to solve or a decision you need to make. Then dismiss it, let it go, and go to sleep. You may find in the morning that you wake up with an answer in your mind.

3. Participate with others in a group meditation. A leader may briefly suggest directions for the group's thought, but should leave plenty of silent

time for the group's thought to work. One pattern goes like this:

- Let us center ourselves on that still point deep within, where we are whole and one with all that is. [Allow a minute or two of silence.]
- Let us feel in harmony with one another and with nature all around. [Silence]
- Let us be aware of the Great Souls—the sages, saints, and seers—who throughout history have guided and guarded humanity and dedicated themselves to the service of the world. [Silence]
- Let us open our hearts and minds to the Light of compassion and wisdom, of creative power and peace, which shines through everything they do, that it may be reflected into our lives and through us to all around. [Silence]
- Let us offer ourselves as a channel of helping and healing for all who are in special need of wholeness, particularly . . . [Names and silence]
- Peace to all beings.

There is one Mind. It is absolutely omni-present, giving mentality to all things.
— Giordano Bruno

Who you think you are is not who you are. You are this vast, limitless, radiant consciousness.
— Gangaji

That which is neither Spirit nor Matter, neither Light nor Darkness, but is verily the container and root of these, that thou art.
— Arysangha

Chapter Twelve

THE SECRET OF
PEACE OF MIND

CHAPTER SUMMARY

*Happiness and peace of mind come from the realization
that we are one with all others as expressions of the
One Life, the One Self, and from the practical application of that realization in a life of service by action
and thought.*

W E CAN LEARN to use the great mental forces that
lie within all of us and to use them to the best
possible effect. As we use them they will grow, until
we find, with surprise and delight, how great a power of
service we wield.

We are continually using these powers unconsciously, spasmodically, feebly, affecting for good or ill all who
cross our path in life. We can also use these same forces

consciously, steadily, and strongly. We cannot avoid thinking, in one way or another, however strong or weak the
thought currents we generate. We inevitably affect those
around us, whether we wish to or not. The only question
is whether we do it harmfully or beneficially, feebly or
strongly, idly or purposefully.

We cannot prevent the thoughts of others from
touching our minds. But we can choose which thoughts
we will receive and which we will reject. We must affect
and be affected, but we may affect others for their benefit or their harm, as we ourselves may be affected for good
or for ill. Here lies our choice, a choice momentous for
ourselves and for the world:

> Choose well; for your choice
> Is brief and yet endless.

All of us, by the choices we make, help to determine
the world of the present and the future. Our choices
therefore have endless consequences. Jiddu Krishnamurti
gave a collection of talks at American universities that
were published under the title *You Are the World*. The
Biblical Book of Proverbs (23.7) says that as we think, so
are we. But because we are the world, as we think, so will
the world be.

The Foundation of Peace

Much of what has already been stated here tells us
something about the way we can ensure peace of mind.
But another factor is fundamental to peace—a clear recognition and realization of our place in the universe. We
are part of one great Life, which knows no failure, no loss

of effort or strength, which "mightily and sweetly order-
ing all things," carries the worlds onward to their goal. The
notion that our personal life is a separate independent
unit, fighting on its own against countless other separate
independent units, is a delusion of the most misleading
kind. As long as we see ourselves, other beings, and the
world around us in that way, peace is far off and inaccessible. But when we feel and know that all selves are one,
then peace of mind without fear of loss is ours.

All our troubles come from thinking of ourselves as
separated units, revolving on our own mental axes, thinking only of our separate interests, our separate aims, our
separate joys and sorrows. Those who think like this with
regard to material things are the most dissatisfied of all
persons, for they restlessly snatch at material goods and
pile up useless treasures for themselves. Others, good
earnest people, may seek their own separate progress
in the higher life, but they too remain discontent and
anxious. They are forever contemplating and analyzing
themselves: "How am I progressing? Am I better than I
was last year?" and so on. They want to be assured of their
progress. Their thoughts are always centered on their own
inner gain.

Peace is not to be found by continually seeking gratification for the separated self, even gratification of a higher kind. It is found in recognizing that the apparently
separated self is really an expression of the Self that is
One. That Self is manifesting at every stage of evolution,
in our present stage as much as in any other. And that Self
is content in all stages; when we recognize our union in it,
we will be content as well.

Desire for spiritual progress is of value while the
lower desires entangle and fetter us. We gain strength to

become free from those lower desires by a passionate longing for spiritual growth. But such longing does not, and cannot, give happiness. We find happiness only when we no longer cling to the separate self and recognize the great Self as what we live for in the world. Even in ordinary life, unselfish people who work to make others happy and forget themselves are happiest. Dissatisfied people are those who constantly seek happiness for themselves.

We are the Self, and therefore the joys and the sorrows of others are ours as much as theirs. To the extent that we realize this and learn to live so that we share the life that flows through us with the whole world—to that extent we learn the secret of peace. That secret is knowledge of the Self, and the thought "That Self am I" (even if we have not yet experienced the reality) helps us to gain a peace of mind that nothing can disturb. As the Bhagavad Gita (2.70) says: "He attains peace, into whom all desires flow as rivers flow into the ocean, which is filled with water, but remains unmoved—not he who desires desire."

My existence does not depend on the fact that I am thinking; it depends on the fact that, whether I know it or not, I am being thought—being thought by a mind much greater than the consciousness which I ordinarily identify with myself.
—Aldous Huxley

APPLICATIONS

1. Think of the web of people and circumstances that brought your breakfast cereal to your table: the grain growing on a farm; the soil, rain, and sun it needs for life; the farm workers; truck drivers; mill and factory workers; advertising specialists; sales clerks; and so on. Work out a similar web for the box the cereal comes in. Contemplate how your life and sustenance depend on many such webs of interaction, how the Earth and everything on it is related.

2. The following is Annie Besant's Universal Invocation. Repeat it to yourself once a day and say it with others when opportunity arises, using it as a focus of thought to send to the world:

> O hidden life, vibrant in every atom,
> O hidden light, shining in every creature,
> O hidden love, embracing all in oneness,
> May all who feel themselves as one with thee
> Know they are therefore one with every other.

> Peace to All Beings.

References and Additional Readings

Bendit, Phoebe. *Our Psychic Sense: A Clairvoyant and a Psychiatrist Explain How It Develops*. Wheaton, IL: Theosophical Publishing House, 1984.

Besant, Annie, trans. *The Bhagavad Gita; or, The Lord's Song*. Adyar, Madras: Theosophical Publishing House, 1974.

————. *Death and After*. Theosophical Manual No. 3. Adyar, Madras: Theosophical Publishing House, 1893.

————. *Karma*. Theosophical Manual No. 4. Adyar, Madras: Theosophical Publishing House, 1895.

————. *Man and His Bodies*. Theosophical Manual No. 7. Adyar, Madras: Theosophical Publishing House, 1896.

————. *The Seven Principles of Man*. Adyar, Madras: Theosophical Publishing House, 1972.

————. *A Study in Consciousness*. Adyar, Madras: Theosophical Publishing House, 1967.

————, and C. W. Leadbeater. *Thought Forms*. Wheaton, IL: Theosophical Publishing House, 1986.

Bhagavan Das. *The Science of the Emotions*. Adyar, Madras, India: Theosophical Publishing House, 1953.

Blavatsky, Helena Petrovna. *The Key to Theosophy*. Ed. Joy Mills. Wheaton, IL: Theosophical Publishing House, 1992. Sections 6 and 10.

———. *The Secret Doctrine*. 3 vols. Wheaton, IL: Theosophical Publishing House, 1993.

Codd, Clara. *Meditation; Its Practice and Results*. Adyar, Madras: Theosophical Publishing House, 1994.

Ellwood, Robert. *Finding the Quiet Mind*. Wheaton, IL: Theosophical Publishing House, 1987.

Gardner, Adelaide. *Meditation: A Practical Study*. Wheaton, IL: Theosophical Publishing House, 1973.

Hanson, Virginia, ed. *Approaches to Meditation*. Wheaton, IL: Theosophical Publishing House, 1976.

———, comp. *Gifts of the Lotus*. Wheaton, IL: Theosophical Publishing House, 1988.

Krishnamurti, Jiddu. *You Are the World*. New York: Harper & Row, 1973.

Kunz, Dora van Gelder. *The Personal Aura*. Wheaton, IL: Theosophical Publishing House, 1991.

Leadbeater, C. W. *The Life after Death*. Adyar, Madras: Theosophical Publishing House, 1994.

———. *Man, Visible and Invisible*. Wheaton, IL: Theosophical Publishing House, 1987.

Sheldrake, Rupert. "Telepathic Telephone Calls: Two Surveys." *Journal of the Society for Psychical Research* 64 (2000): 224–32.

Taimni, I. K. *A Way to Self-Discovery*. Wheaton, IL: Theosophical Publishing House, 1970.

Wood, Ernest. *Concentration: An Approach to Meditation*. Wheaton, IL: Theosophical Publishing House, 1994.

INDEX

This index includes proper names, foreign words, subjects, and key terms. For the last, only characteristic or defining contexts are indexed, because many of the terms occur frequently throughout the book.

Printed in the United States
204286BV00005B/89/P